TAKING SIDES

Library Index
and
Guide

*An index to the tables of contents, issues, and topics
in the fourteen-volume library set.*

DPG

The Dushkin Publishing Group, Inc.

Taking Sides® is a registered trademark of
The Dushkin Publishing Group, Inc.

Manufactured in the United States of America

ISBN: 0-87967-826-7

PREFACE

The **Taking Sides Library** is an easy-to-access source of lively and thought provoking controversial issues from a wide range of disciplines. These controversies can be used as the basis for term papers, brief writing assignments, in-class debates or discussions, speech contests—any situation where a stimulating and critical examination of a topic is required.

The **Taking Sides Library** is comprised of fourteen debate style readers. Each reader is designed to introduce students to a mix of long-standing and contemporary controversies within a field of study. A question is asked (e.g., *Should Capital Punishment Be Abolished?*), and an affirmative and a negative response is supplied (e.g., *Yes: Jack Greenberg* from "Against the American System of Capital Punishment"/*No: Ernest van den Haag*, from "The Ultimate Punishment: A Defense"). The **Taking Sides Library** has a total of 514 pro-con essays that debate 257 important issues.

The purpose of the debate format is to stimulate interest in the subject matter and to encourage critical thinking. The pro and con essays reflect a variety of ideological viewpoints and are selected for their liveliness and because of their value in a debate framework. The selections are written by scholars and commentators who are respected and accomplished in their fields.

Each issue in each of the volumes in the **Taking Sides Library** has an issue introduction, which sets the stage for the debate, provides some background information on each author, and generally puts the issue into context. Each issue concludes with a postscript that briefly summarizes the debate, gives the reader paths for further investigation, and suggests additional readings that might be helpful. Each volume in the **Taking Sides Library** concludes with a list of Contributors (with a brief biography of each contributor) and an Index. (See Explanatory Chart on next page.)

How to Use This *Library Index and Guide*

This *Library Index and Guide* is designed to be a quick and easy reference to the issues in each of the *Taking Sides* volumes. It has four sections:

- Reference Key
- Tables of Contents
- Issue List
- Topic Index

EXPLANATORY CHART

Issue Introduction

Postscript

ISSUE 3
Do Political Action Committees Undermine Democracy?

POSTSCRIPT

YES: Fred Wertheimer, from "Campaign Finance Reform: The Unfinished Agenda," *Annals of the American Academy* (July, 1986)

NO: Phyllis Schlafly, from "PACs Protect Political Participation," *The Phyllis Schlafly Report* (August, 1986)

ISSUE SUMMARY

YES: Common Cause President Fred Wertheimer argues that PACs exert too much influence over the electoral process, allowing special interests to get the ear of elected officials at the expense of the national interest.
NO: Conservative activist Phyllis Schlafly defends PACs because they are a means of exercising the right to free speech and because they permit conservative voices to be heard during political campaigns.

Do Political Action Committees Undermine Democracy?

Half a century ago, American folk humorist Will Rogers observed that it took a lot of money even to *lose* an election. What would Will Rogers say if he were alive today?

The cost of television as a medium of communication and persuasion has greatly increased the expenditures in election campaigns. In 1984, campaign expenditures for the presidential election totaled $325 million, $50 million more than in the previous election. Campaign spending on House and Senate races totaled $450 million in 1986, more than double the amount spent in 1978. Money, said a prominent California politician, is the "mother's milk of politics."

More controversial than the amount of money spent in politics is its source. Political action committees have become a major factor in financing American election campaigns. PACs (as they are called) have proliferated in recent years, with more than one hundred new special-interest groups being founded each year. It is estimated that there are now more than 4,100 PACs, representing almost every conceivable political interest.

By raising money from political sympathizers, association members, and public solicitations, PACs have provided the funds with which candidates reach the public. It is estimated that PACs spent more than $80 million on campaigns in 1982, when there was no presidential election. In 1984 at least

Interestingly, both Schlafly and Wertheimer claim to be defending democratic values—and perhaps they both are. Schlafly looks at democracy in terms of participation, and she sees PACs as a means of getting more people involved in the electoral process. Wertheimer emphasizes the need for equality in the democratic process, and he worries that PACs make some voters "more equal" than others.

Edward Roeder has edited a useful directory of PACs that supplies information about their sources, their funds, and whom they support. See his *PACs Americana: The Directory of Political Action Committees and Their Interests*, 2nd ed. (Sunshine Service, 1986). Larry Sabato's *PAC Power* (Norton, 1984) is a comprehensive overview of PACs: what they are, how they operate, and their impact. Frank J. Sorauf's *What Price PACs?* (Priority Press, 1985) studies PAC financing and its implications today. For an excellent general study of interest groups, including PACs, see Graham K. Wilson, *Interest Groups in the United States* (Clarendon Press, 1981).

Other countries succeed in setting strict limits on campaign spending. Can we do it without inhibiting political expression? Should we substitute public financing of congressional elections? Or do we accept PACs as a vigorous expression of political freedom? In short, do PACs undermine or do they underline democracy?

38

51

The Reference Key provides an explanation for the abbreviations used for the *Taking Sides* titles. The Tables of Contents section reproduces the detailed table of contents from each *Taking Sides* volume. The Issue List is an alphabetical listing of every issue, and each issue is cross-referenced to the *Taking Sides* volume in which it appears. In the Topic Index, each issue in the 14 volumes that comprise the **Taking Sides Library** has been indexed according to its main topic(s) and is cross-referenced to the *Taking Sides* volume in which it appears. (See sample entry from the Issue List on p. 92 and from the Topic Index on p. 100.)

Once you have located an issue of interest in the Issue List or Topic Index, you can easily turn to the Tables of Contents sections, locate the table of

Contributors

Index

AUTHORS

HARRY BLACKMUN is associate justice of the U.S. Supreme Court. He was appointed in 1970 by President Nixon.

WILLIAM J. BRENNAN, Jr., is associate justice of the U.S. Supreme Court. He was appointed in 1956 by President Eisenhower.

NOAM CHOMSKY is the Institute Professor in the Department of Linguistics and Philosophy at the Massachusetts Institute of Technology.

GEORGE COWLEY is a staff writer for the *Seattle Weekly.*

BARRY CRICKMER is a senior editor of *Nation's Business,* a monthly magazine published by the Chamber of Commerce of the United States.

EDD DOERR is executive director of Americans for Religious Liberty in Silver Spring, Maryland.

G. WILLIAM DOMHOFF is professor of psychology and sociology at the University of California, Santa Cruz.

GREGG EASTERBROOK is a writer who contributes regularly to *The Atlantic Monthly, Newsweek,* and other publications.

MARK FALCOFF was a senior consultant to the Kissinger Commis-

sion on Central America and a professional staff member with the Senate Foreign Relations Committee in the 99th Congress.

JOHN LEWIS GADDIS is professor of history at Ohio University.

GEORGE GOLDBERG is an author and member of the New York State Bar.

BARRY GOLDWATER was U.S. senator from Arizona from 1953–1965, and from 1969–1987.

ANDREW GREELEY is a Roman Catholic priest and professor of sociology at the University of Arizona.

LOIS HAIGNERE is a research associate and assistant director of the New York State Comparable Pay Study at the Center for Women at the State University of New York at Albany.

BEVERLY W. HARRISON is professor of Christian ethics at the Union Theological Seminary in New York.

EDWARD S. HERMAN is professor of finance at the Wharton School of Business at the University of Pennsylvania.

HENRY J. HYDE is a Republican congressman from Illinois.

Grigsby, Shaw, 189
Griswold v. Connecticut, 248, 249, 253
Guatemala: 301; biased news coverage of, 61–62, 65

Haignere, Lois, on comparable worth, 214–218
halfway house(s), as alternative to prisons, 173
Hart, Gary: 98, 219, 222; on role of Political Action Committees in financing campaigns, 41
Hatch Amendment, 267
health and safety regulation, failure of, 120, 121, 122, 123
hearings, television coverage of congressional, 75
Herman, Edward S., on media propaganda, 60–65
heroin, 159, 160
holiday observances, school, and religion in public education, 284
homosexuals, issue of constitutional rights of, 246–255
homosexual sodomy, controversy over criminalizing of, 248–255
Honduras, 299, 301, 305
humanism, and controversy over religion in public education, 278, 281, 282
Humanist Manifesto I, 282
Humanist Manifesto II, 282
Hyde, Henry J., on eliminating religious values from public life, 269–274

Immigration, impact of Mexican, on United States, 312, 313
impeachment, of a Supreme Court justice, 140
incarceration: alternatives to, 173–175; United States rate of, 169, 170
incorporation doctrine, and Supreme Court, 140
incumbents, advantages of, 42, 48
intensive-supervision probation, as alternative to prison, 173
intercontinental missiles, and United States foreign policy in Central America, 309, 310

Javits, Jacob K., on War Powers Resolution, 110–115
Jefferson, Thomas, 108, 109
Jim Crow, 203
job content analysis, and pay equity, 216, 220, 221, 222
Job Corps, 163
job creation, effect of, on crime rates, 158, 161, 162
job evaluation, and pay equity issue, 215–217, 220–222
joblessness: black male, 239–244; role of, in labor force, 238, 239, 243

job training: effect of, on crime, 163; and welfare issue, 233
Johnston, Jerry, 283
jury, and imposing the death penalty, 183
just compensation, 145
justice, and argument for capital punishment, 181, 182

Katz v. United States, 252, 254
Kayden, Xandra, on role of political parties today, 29–36
Kennedy, Paul, on relationship of fall of major powers and shift in economic strength, 344–352
Khrushchev, Nikita, 331, 332
King, Martin Luther, Jr., 207, 210
Klitgaard, Robert, 200

labor force participation, black vs. white, and welfare, 238–240
labor-management relations, and comparable worth issue, 223
"lack of opportunities," as cause of crime, 164
Laski, Harold, 187
Latin America, controversy over United States involvement in, 298–316
Law Enforcement Assistance Administration, (LEAA), 174
Law of the Sea, 312
lawyers, as elected officials, 7
legalized abortion: 142; and religious values of public officials, 264–269, 271, 272
legislature: influence of Political Action Committee contributions on, 40–50, *see also,* Congress
lex talionis, 187
liberals: news media as biased toward, 54–59; view of Political Action Committees by, 44, 46–48; of Supreme Court, 139, 140
lobbyists: denial of Access to Capitol to, 81; increased number of, 73; multiple, 77–78
local political parties, decline in role of, 29–32
Loury, Glenn C., on civil rights strategies as threat to full equality of blacks and whites, 198–204
Loving v. Virginia, 254
Lowenthal, Abraham F., on U.S. foreign aid in Central America, 308–316
low-income families, black, and welfare system, 238, 239

MacNamara, Donal E. J., and argument against capital punishment, 187–194
Madison, James, 145
Mahe, Eddie, Jr., on role of political parties today, 29–36
male marriageable pool index (MMPI), and welfare system, 239, 240, 242–244

contents for the *Taking Sides* volume in which your issue appears, and read a brief description of the issue. In this way, the *Library Index and Guide* quickly gives you access to information on a controversial issue, and you can more accurately target the most appropriate volume (or volumes) for your needs.

We hope that you will find this *Library Guide and Index* to be a valuable reference tool. Please let us know how it can be improved.

Marguerite L. Egan
Program Manager

CONTENTS

Preface i

Reference Key 1

Tables of Contents 2
    American History, vol. 1, Third Edition **2**
    American History, vol. 2, Third Edition **8**
    Bioethical, Third Edition **14**
    Crime and Criminology, First Edition **21**
    Economic, Fourth Edition **27**
    Education, Fifth Edition **34**
    Environmental, Third Edition **40**
    Human Sexuality, Second Edition **47**
    Legal, Third Edition **55**
    Moral, First Edition **60**
    Political, Sixth Edition **66**
    Psychological, Fifth Edition **72**
    Social, Fifth Edition **78**
    World Politics, Second Edition **84**

Issue List 91

Topic Index 99

REFERENCE KEY

Use the following key to determine the *Taking Sides* volume references used in this index:

AH1   *Taking Sides: Clashing Views on Controversial Issues in American History, Volume One*, Third edition

AH2   *Taking Sides: Clashing Views on Controversial Issues in American History, Volume Two*, Third edition

Bio   *Taking Sides: Clashing Views on Controversial Bioethical Issues*, Third edition

CR   *Taking Sides: Clashing Views on Controversial Issues in Crime and Criminology*, First edition

Eco   *Taking Sides: Clashing Views on Controversial Economic Issues*, Fourth edition

Edu   *Taking Sides: Clashing Views on Controversial Educational Issues*, Fifth edition

Env   *Taking Sides: Clashing Views on Controversial Environmental Issues*, Third edition

HS   *Taking Sides: Clashing Views on Controversial Issues in Human Sexuality*, Second edition

Leg   *Taking Sides: Clashing Views on Controversial Legal Issues*, Third edition

Mor   *Taking Sides: Clashing Views on Controversial Moral Issues*, First edition

Pol   *Taking Sides: Clashing Views on Controversial Political Issues*, Sixth edition

Psy   *Taking Sides: Clashing Views on Controversial Psychological Issues*, Fifth edition

Soc   *Taking Sides: Clashing Views on Controversial Social Issues*, Fifth edition

WP   *Taking Sides: Clashing Views on Controversial Issues in World Politics*, Second edition

AMERICAN HISTORY, Volume One, Third Edition

ISSUE 1. Was Colonial American Culture Unique?   **2**

YES: Gary B. Nash, from *Race, Class, and Politics: Essays on American Colonial and Revolutionary Society*   **4**

NO: Carlton J. H. Hayes, from "The American Frontier—Frontier of What?" *American Historical Review*   **11**

Nash argues that colonial American culture developed from a convergence of three broad cultural traditions—European, Native American, and African—which produced a unique tri-racial society in the New World. Hayes views American society as a New World extension of the traditions of European or Western culture.

ISSUE 2. Was Conflict Unavoidable Between Native Americans and Colonists?   **20**

YES: Alden T. Vaughan, from "White Man to Redskin: Changing Anglo-American Perceptions of the American Indians," *American Historical Review*   **22**

NO: Richard R. Johnson, from "The Search for a Usable Indian: An Aspect of the Defense of Colonial New England," *Journal of American History*   **29**

Vaughan presents the Native American as a victim of color symbolism, racial differences, and nonconformity to European cultural traditions. Johnson chronicles cooperative relations between settlers and natives in the New World.

ISSUE 3. Was the Colonial Period a "Golden Age" for Women in America?   **36**

YES: Lois Green Carr and Lorena S. Walsh, from "The Planter's Wife: The Experience of White Women in Seventeenth-Century Maryland," *William and Mary Quarterly*   **38**

NO: Lyle Koehler, from *A Search for Power: The "Weaker Sex" in Seventeenth-Century New England*   **46**

Carr and Walsh identify several factors that coalesced in the seventeenth century to afford women in Maryland a higher status with fewer restraints

on their social conduct than those experienced by women in England. Koehler contends that the division of labor that separated work into male and female spheres and Puritan attitudes towards rights of inheritance severely limited opportunities for upward mobility among New England women.

ISSUE 4. Did American Slaves Develop a Distinct Afro-American Culture in the Eighteenth Century? 56

YES: Allan Kulikoff, from *Tobacco and Slaves: The Development of Southern Cultures in the Chesapeake, 1680–1800* 58

NO: Jean Butenhoff Lee, from "The Problem of Slave Community in the Eighteenth-Century Chesapeake," *William and Mary Quarterly* 67

Kulikoff claims that Chesapeake slaves developed their own social institutions and a distinct indigenous culture in the half century between 1740 and 1790. Lee emphasizes the difficult and often unsuccessful efforts of slaves to create and maintain a stable family and community life in eighteenth-century Maryland.

ISSUE 5. Was the Great Awakening a Key to the American Revolution? 78

YES: William G. McLoughlin, from " 'Enthusiasm for Liberty': The Great Awakening as the Key to the Revolution," in Greene and McLoughlin, *Preachers and Politicians: Two Essays on the Origins of the American Revolution* 80

NO: Jon Butler, from "Enthusiasm Described and Decried: The Great Awakening as Interpretative Fiction," *Journal of American History* 88

McLoughlin claims that the Great Awakening, by promoting religious revitalization, intercolonial unity, and democracy, paved the way for the American Revolution. Butler challenges the validity of the term "the Great Awakening" and argues that a link between the eighteenth-century colonial religious revivals and the American Revolution was virtually nonexistent.

ISSUE 6. Can the Revolution Serve as a Developmental Model for Third World Nations Today? 102

YES: Richard B. Morris, from *The Emerging Nations and the American Revolution* 104

NO: Carl N. Degler, from "The American Past: An Unsuspected Obstacle in Foreign Affairs," *American Scholar* 111

Historian Richard F. Morris argues that the American Revolution was both a war of decolonization and a movement of wide-ranging political, social, and

economic changes. Pulitzer Prize-winning author Carl N. Degler believes that, because of its unique conservative attempt to maintain the "status quo," the American Revolution is meaningless as a model for Third World nations to imitate.

ISSUE 7. The Constitution: Was It an Economic Document?   124

YES: Michael Parenti, from *Democracy for the Few,* 5th ed.   126

NO: Henry Steele Commager, from *The Search for a Usable Past*   136

Political scientist Michael Parenti argues that the Constitution was framed by financially successful planters, merchants, and creditors in order to protect the rights of property ahead of the rights and liberties of persons. Well-known essayist and historian Henry Steele Commager maintains the Constitution was essentially a political document designed to solve the problem of the distribution of power between the national government *and* the state and local governments.

ISSUE 8. Did President Jefferson Outfederalize the Federalists?   148

YES: Richard Hofstadter, from "Thomas Jefferson: The Aristocrat as Democrat," *The American Political Tradition and the Men Who Made It*   150

NO: Forrest McDonald, from *The Presidency of Thomas Jefferson*   162

Pulitzer Prize-winning historian Hofstadter argues that Thomas Jefferson was a moderate, practical politician who followed a course of action which eventually co-opted the major policies of the Federalists. Professor Forrest McDonald believes that President Jefferson attempted to replace Hamiltonian Federalist principles with a Republican ideology and wanted to restore America's agrarian heritage.

ISSUE 9. Did Women Achieve Greater Autonomy in the New Nation?   176

YES: Nancy Woloch, from *Women and the American Experience*   178

NO: Gerda Lerner, from "The Lady and the Mill Girl: Changes in Status of Women in the Age of Jackson," *American Studies Journal*   189

Woloch describes the exercise of autonomy and authority in the domestic life of middle-class wives. Lerner considers a spectrum of women's roles, emphasizing the subservient position of female industrial workers.

ISSUE 10. Did the Election of 1828 Represent a Democratic Revolt of the People?   **200**

YES: Robert V. Remini, from "Election of 1828," Arthur Schlesinger, Jr., ed., *The Coming to Power*   **202**

NO: Richard P. McCormick, from "New Perspectives on Jacksonian Politics," *American Historical Review*   **207**

Professor Robert V. Remini argues that the 1828 presidential election symbolized the people's arrival at political responsibility and began a genuine, nationally organized, two-party system that came of age in the 1830s. Historian Richard P. McCormick maintains that voting statistics demonstrate that a genuine political revolution did not take place until the presidential elections of 1840, when fairly well-balanced political parties had been organized in virtually every state.

ISSUE 11. Was Antebellum Reform Motivated Primarily by Humanitarian Goals?   **214**

YES: Alice Felt Tyler, from *Freedom's Ferment: Phases of America's Social History from the Colonial Period to the Outbreak of the Civil War*   **216**

NO: Michael B. Katz, from "Poorhouses and the Origins of the Public Old Age Home," *Milbank Memorial Fund Quarterly*   **224**

Tyler argues that American reformers in the antebellum period were products of frontier democracy and evangelical religion who accepted a mission of perfecting human institutions. Katz contends that poorhouses were established not only to provide a refuge for the helpless but also to encourage the Protestant work ethic by deterring members of the working class from seeking poor relief.

ISSUE 12. Was U.S. Foreign Policy in the Early Nineteenth Century Imperialistic?   **236**

YES: Ramon Eduardo Ruiz, from "Manifest Destiny and the Mexican War," Quint et al., eds., *Major Problems in American History, vol. 1, 5th ed.*   **238**

NO: Robert Hugh Ferrell, from *American Diplomacy, A History, 2d ed.*   **246**

Professor Ramon E. Ruiz argues that for the purpose of conquering Mexico's northern territories, the United States waged against Mexico an aggressive war from which she never recovered. Diplomatic historian Robert Ferrell, however, believes that although the American government waged an aggres-

sive war in Mexico, it remained the manifest destiny of the United States to possess Texas, New Mexico, and California.

ISSUE 13. Did Slavery Destroy the Black Family?   256

YES: Kenneth M. Stampp, from *The Peculiar Institution: Slavery in the Ante-Bellum South*   258

NO: Leslie Howard Owens, from *This Species of Property: Slave Life and Other Culture in the Old South*   266

Stampp contends that the master's absolute power prevented slaves from establishing and maintaining stable family units. Owens recognizes the threats to family stability among slaves but emphasizes the relentless efforts of fathers, mothers, and children to achieve family unity within the slave quarters.

ISSUE 14. Were the Abolitionists "Unrestrained Fanatics"?   278

YES: Avery Craven, from *The Coming of the Civil War,* 2d ed.   280

NO: Irving H. Bartlett, from "The Persistence of Wendell Phillips," Martin Duberman, ed., *The Antislavery Vanguard: New Essays on the Abolitionists*   288

Craven believes that the fanaticism of the abolitionist crusade created an atmosphere of crisis that resulted in the outbreak of the Civil War. Bartlett differentiates between agitation and fanaticism and claims that abolitionists like Wendell Phillips were deeply committed to improving the quality of life for all Americans, including those blacks held as slaves.

ISSUE 15. Was the Antebellum South a Unique Section in American History?   298

YES: Eugene D. Genovese, from *The Political Economy of Slavery*   300

NO: Edward Pessen, from "How Different From Each Other Were the Antebellum North and South?" *American Historical Review*   314

Marxist historian Eugene D. Genovese believes "that slavery gave the South a social system and a civilization with a distinct class structure, political community, economy, ideology, and set of psychological patterns." Social historian Edward Pessen argues that a comparison of Northern and Southern states in the three decades before the Civil War reveals common political, economic, and social practices.

ISSUE 16. Was Abraham Lincoln America's Greatest President?   330

YES: Stephen B. Oates, from *Abraham Lincoln: The Man Behind the Myths*   332

NO: M. E. Bradford, from *Remembering Who We Are: Observations of a Southern Conservative*   342

Oates insists that Abraham Lincoln's greatness as president of the United States stemmed from a moral vision that had as its goal the protection and expansion of popular government. Bradford characterizes Lincoln as a cynical politician whose abuse of authority as president and commander-in-chief during the Civil War marked a serious departure from the republican goals of the Founding Fathers and established the prototype for the "imperial presidency" of the twentieth century.

ISSUE 17. Was Reconstruction a Total Failure?   352

YES: J. G. Randall, from *The Civil War and Reconstruction*   354

NO: Eric Foner, from "The New View of Reconstruction," *American Heritage*   360

Randall argues that Reconstruction failed because carpetbaggers and their "Negro" allies misgoverned the South and looted its treasuries. Foner believes that, although Reconstruction was nonrevolutionary and conservative, it was a splendid failure because it offered blacks a temporary vision of a free society.

AMERICAN HISTORY,
Volume Two, Third Edition

ISSUE 1. Was Reconstruction a Total Failure?   2

YES: J. G. Randall, from *The Civil War and Reconstruction*   4

NO: Eric Foner, from "The New View of Reconstruction," *American Heritage*   10

Randall argues that Reconstruction failed because carpetbaggers and their "Negro" allies misgoverned the South and looted its treasuries. Professor Eric Foner believes that, although Reconstruction was nonrevolutionary and conservative, it was a splendid failure because it offered blacks a temporary vision of a free society.

ISSUE 2. Was John D. Rockefeller a "Robber Baron"?   22

YES: Matthew Josephson, from *The Robber Barons*   24

NO: Maury Klein, from "The Robber Barons: Many May Not Have Deserved the Title," *American History Illustrated*   32

Social critic Matthew Josephson believes that John D. Rockefeller was the classic example of a monopoly capitalist who utilized ruthless and violent methods in organizing the oil industry. Historian Maury Klein maintains that Rockefeller was a successful industrial statesman who, with ruthless brilliance, organized the chaotic oil industry into a horizontally and vertically integrated empire, which stimulated the development of many new industries.

ISSUE 3. Was the American Labor Movement Radical?   44

YES: Leon Fink, from *Workingmen's Democracy: The Knights of Labor and American Politics*   46

NO: Carl N. Degler, from *Out of Our Past: The Forces That Shaped Modern America*, 3d ed.   58

Though stopping short of a frontal attack on capitalism, Professor Leon Fink argues that the Knights of Labor envisioned a kind of workingman's democracy that would ensure minimal standards of health and safety in the industrial workplace. Historian Carl N. Degler maintains that the American

labor movement accepted capitalism and reacted conservatively to the radical organizational changes brought about in the economic system by big business.

ISSUE 4. Were the Immigrants' Old World Cultures Destroyed as They Adjusted to American Life? 68

YES: Oscar Handlin, from *The Uprooted: The Epic Story of the People of the Great Migrations That Made the American People,* 2d ed. 70

NO: John Bodnar, from *The Transplanted: A History of Immigrants in Urban America* 78

Oscar Handlin argues that the immigrants were alienated from their Old World cultures as they adjusted to an unfamiliar and hostile environment. John Bodnar maintains that various immigrant groups retained, modified, and transformed their Old World cultures in responding to urban-industrial America in the years between 1880 and 1920.

ISSUE 5. Were the Populists Democratic Reformers? 92

YES: Lawrence Goodwyn, from *Democratic Promise: The Populist Moment in America* 94

NO: Richard Hofstadter, from *The Age of Reform: From Bryan to F.D.R.* 100

Goodwyn defines Populism as a cooperative "people's movement" that sought to take control of the government in order to fulfill mass democratic aspirations. Hofstadter focuses upon the nostalgic, reactionary nature of the Populists, whose attitudes revealed a desire to create a rural utopia, using the early nineteenth-century United States as their model.

ISSUE 6. Was City Government in Late Nineteenth-Century America a "Conspicuous Failure"? 110

YES: Ernest S. Griffith, from *A History of American City Government: The Conspicuous Failure, 1870–1900* 112

NO: Jon C. Teaford, from *The Unheralded Triumph: City Government in America, 1870–1900* 121

Griffith focuses upon illegal and unethical operations of the political machine and concludes that the governments controlled by the bosses represented a betrayal of the public trust. Teaford argues that scholars traditionally have overlooked the remarkable success municipal governments in the late nineteenth century achieved in dealing with the challenges presented by rapid urbanization.

ISSUE 7. Did the Progressives Fail?   132

YES: Richard M. Abrams, from "The Failure of Progressivism," Richard Abrams and Lawrence Levine, eds., *The Shaping of the Twentieth Century*, 2d ed.   134

NO: Arthur S. Link and Richard L. McCormick, from *Progressivism*   144

Professor Richard Abrams maintains that progressivism was a failure because it tried to impose a uniform set of values upon a culturally diverse people and never seriously confronted the inequalities which still exist in American society. Professors Arthur S. Link and Richard L. McCormick argue that the progressives were a diverse group of reformers who confronted and ameliorated the worst abuses which emerged in urban-industrial America during the early 1900s.

ISSUE 8. Was U.S. Intervention in Nicaragua in the Early Twentieth Century Motivated by "Dollar Diplomacy"?   158

YES: Walter LaFeber, from *Inevitable Revolutions: The United States in Central America*   160

NO: Samuel Flagg Bemis, from *The Latin American Policy of the United States*   174

Professor Walter LaFeber argues that the United Stated developed a foreign policy which deliberately made the Caribbean nations its economic dependents from the early nineteenth century. Professor Samuel Flagg Bemis maintains that U. S. interventions in the Caribbean led to a short-lived period of "benevolent imperialism," which gave political and economic stability to the area and at the same time prevented European intervention in its internal affairs.

ISSUE 9. Did Woodrow Wilson Fail as Commander-in-Chief During World War I?   186

YES: George F. Kennan, from *American Diplomacy: 1900–1950*   188

NO: D. F. Trask, from "Woodrow Wilson and the Reconciliation of Force and Diplomacy, 1917–1918" *Naval War College Review*   196

Former diplomat and historian George F. Kennan believes that President Wilson was an impractical idealist who led America into the right war for the wrong reasons. Historian David F. Trask argues Wilson developed realistic and clearly articulated war goals and coordinated his larger diplomatic aims with the use of force better than any other wartime American president.

ISSUE 10. Did The Women's Movement Die in the 1920s?   208
YES: Lois W. Banner, from *Women in Modern America: A Brief History* 210
NO: Anne Firor Scott, from *The Southern Lady: From Pedestal to Politics, 1830–1930*   220

Banner concludes that, following the ratification of the Nineteenth Amendment, antifeminist trends combined with a lack of unity among women's organizations to hinder further progress on women's issues in the 1920s. Scott insists that the suffrage victory produced a heightened interest in further social and political reform, which inspired Southern women to pursue these goals throughout the 1920s.

ISSUE 11. Was the New Deal an Effective Answer to the Great Depression?   232
YES: William E. Leuchtenburg, from "The Achievement of the New Deal," Harvard Sitkoff, ed., *Fifty Years Later: The New Deal Evaluated*   234
NO: Brad Wiley, from "The Myth of New Deal Reform," Tom Christoffel et al., *Up Against the American Myth*   245

Professor William E. Leuchtenburg contends that the New Deal extended the power of the national government in order to humanize the worst features of American capitalism. Brad Wiley argues that the New Deal stabilized the corporate-capitalistic system of production and produced only superficial social and economic reforms.

ISSUE 12. Was the Conflict Between the United States and Russia Inevitable?   256
YES: Robert Kelley, from *The Shaping of the American Past*, vol. 2, 4th ed.   258
NO: Thomas G. Paterson, from *Soviet-American Confrontation: Postwar Reconstruction and the Origins of the Cold War*   270

Professor Robert Kelley believes that the conflicting values and goals of a democratic-capitalist United States and a communist Russia after World War II made the Cold War inevitable. Revisionist historian Thomas G. Paterson maintains that the United States used its dominant military and economic power after World War II to reshape the world according to its own views of political democracy and international free trade.

ISSUE 13. Was Dwight Eisenhower a Great President?   284

YES: Stephen E. Ambrose, from *Eisenhower: The President*, vol. 2   286

NO: Arthur M. Schlesinger, Jr., from *The Cycles of American History*   294

Stephen E. Ambrose maintains that Eisenhower is a greater president than his Democratic and Republican predecessors and successors because he balanced the budget, stopped inflation, and kept the peace. Arthur Schlesinger, Jr., argues that Eisenhower failed as a president because he refused to tackle the moral and environmental issues at home and because he established a foreign policy which relied on covert CIA activities and threats of nuclear arms.

ISSUE 14. Could the United States Have Prevented the Fall of South Vietnam?   306

YES: Guenter Lewy, from *America in Vietnam*   308

NO: George C. Herring, from "The 'Vietnam Syndrome' and American Foreign Policy," *Virginia Quarterly Review*   317

Historian Guenter Lewy believes that the South Vietnamese government might not have lost the war if the United States had followed "a strategy of surprise and massed strength at decisive points" against North Vietnam. Historian George Herring argues that the policy makers exaggerated the strategic importance of Vietnam and deluded themselves about America's power.

ISSUE 15. Was Martin Luther King, Jr.'s Leadership Essential to the Success of the Civil Rights Movement?   328

YES: August Meier, from "On the Role of Martin Luther King," Meier and Rudwick, eds., *Along the Color Line: Explorations in the Black Experience*   330

NO: Clayborne Carson, from "Martin Luther King, Jr.: Charismatic Leadership in a Mass Struggle," *Journal of American History*   339

Meier depicts King as a "conservative militant" whose ability to communicate black aspirations to whites and to serve as a bridge between the radical and conservative wings of the civil rights movement made him the critical link in the chain of nonviolent direct action campaigns of the 1960s. Carson concludes that the civil rights struggle would have followed a similar course of development even had King never lived because its successes depended upon mass activism, not the actions of a single leader.

ISSUE 16. Is the United States in a Period of Decline?   346

YES: Paul Kennedy, from *The Rise and Fall of the Great Powers: Economic Change and Military Conflict From 1500 to 2000*   348

NO: Susan Strange, from "The Persistent Myth of Lost Hegemony," *International Organization*   357

Historian Paul Kennedy believes that the United States, like other great nations before it, has declined in power because of its excessive military commitments, its huge federal deficit, and its decreasing share of global production. Political scientist Susan Strange maintains that the United States still possesses the structural power to reshape the global political economy through its military strength, financial clout, control over world knowledge, and production of goods and services.

BIOETHICAL ISSUES,
Third Edition

ISSUE 1. Is Abortion Immoral? 2

YES: John T. Noonan, Jr., from "An Almost Absolute Value in History," *The Morality of Abortion: Legal and Historical Perspectives* 4

NO: Beverly Wildung Harrison, from *Our Right to Choose: Toward a New Ethics of Abortion* 10

Professor of law John T. Noonan, Jr., believes that a fetus is conceived by human parents and that it is just as wrong to destroy its life as it would be to destroy the life of any human. Professor of Christian ethics Beverly Wildung Harrison argues that women ought to decide whether or not to bear children on the basis of their own moral preparedness to become mothers.

ISSUE 2. Is It Wrong to Create Test-Tube Babies? 16

YES: Hans O. Tiefel, from "Human In Vitro Fertilization: A Conservative View," *Journal of the American Medical Association* 18

NO: Clifford Grobstein, from "Coming to Terms with Test-Tube Babies," *New Scientist* 25

Professor of religion Hans O. Tiefel opposes the new technology of in vitro fertilization on the grounds that it may cause harm to both mothers and embryos. Biologist Clifford Grobstein argues that this technology is a useful therapy for infertile couples and that we can avoid potential moral problems by developing sound principles.

ISSUE 3. Should Women Be Allowed to Bear Babies for a Fee? 32

YES: John A. Robertson, from "Surrogate Mothers: Not So Novel After All," *Hastings Center Report* 34

NO: Herbert F. Krimmel, from "The Case Against Surrogate Parenting," *Hastings Center Report* 41

Professor of law John A. Robertson believes that infertile couples have a right to arrange for a surrogate mother to bear the husband's child and that the ethical and legal problems that might result are not very different from those that already exist in adoption and artificial insemination by donor. Professor of law Herbert F. Krimmel takes the position that it is immoral to bear a child

for the purpose of giving it up and that surrogate mother arrangements will put additional strain on our society's shared moral values.

ISSUE 4. Is It Ethical to Withhold the Truth from Dying Patients?   52

YES: Bernard C. Meyer, from "Truth and the Physician," *Ethical Issues in Medicine*   54

NO: Sissela Bok, from *Lying: Moral Choice in Public and Private Life*   65

Physician Bernard C. Meyer argues that physicians must use discretion in communicating bad news to patients. Adherence to a rigid formula of truthtelling fails to appreciate the differences in patients' readiness to hear and understand the information. Philosopher Sissela Bok challenges the traditional physicians' view by arguing that the harm resulting from disclosure is less than they think and is outweighed by the benefits, including the important one of giving the patient the right to choose among treatments.

ISSUE 5. Is "Killing" the Same As "Letting Die"?   76

YES: James Rachels, from "Active and Passive Euthanasia," *New England Journal of Medicine*   78

NO: Tom L. Beauchamp and James F. Childress, from *Principles of Biomedical Ethics*   84

Philosopher James Rachels argues that the conventional distinction between active euthanasia (killing) and passive euthanasia (letting die) has no moral importance. Philosophers Tom L. Beauchamp and James F. Childress hold that the distinction is not only valid morally (it upholds certain principles such as "do no harm") but also practically (it avoids certain harmful consequences, such as loss of patients' trust in physicians).

ISSUE 6. Must Fluids and Nutrition Always Be Given to Dying Patients?   94

YES: William E. May et al., from "Feeding and Hydrating the Permanently Unconscious and Other Vulnerable Persons," *Issues in Law and Medicine*   96

NO: Joanne Lynn and James F. Childress, from "Must Patients Always Be Given Food and Water?" *Hastings Center Report*   102

Professor of moral theology William E. May and colleagues conclude that foods and fluids are universally needed for the preservation of life, and can generally be provided without the burdens of more aggressive means of supporting life. Physician Joanne Lynn and professor of religious studies

James F. Childress claim that nutrition and hydration are not morally different from other life-sustaining medical treatments that may on occasion be withheld or withdrawn, according to the patients' best interests.

ISSUE 7. Should Parents Be Allowed to Decide to Withhold Treatment from Newborns with Birth Defects? 112

YES: Earl E. Shelp, from *Born to Die: Deciding the Fate of Critically Ill Newborns* 114

NO: C. Everett Koop, from "Ethical and Surgical Considerations in the Care of the Newborn with Congenital Abnormalities," *Infanticide and the Handicapped Newborn* 117

Theologian Earl E. Shelp believes that parents should be the ultimate decision-makers about medical treatment for severely diseased or defective newborns. C. Everett Koop, a pediatric surgeon who is now Surgeon General of the United States, calls withholding treatment from newborns "infanticide" and faults the medical profession for acceding to the wishes of the families instead of protecting their patients.

ISSUE 8. Are There Limits to Confidentiality? 126

YES: Ian E. Thompson, from "The Nature of Confidentiality," *Journal of Medical Ethics* 128

NO: Michael H. Kottow, from "Medical Confidentiality: An Intransigent and Absolute Obligation," *Journal of Medical Ethics* 138

Senior educationalist Ian E. Thompson argues that there are exceptions to practically any code of rules, including confidentiality. Very little may be truly confidential in the doctor-patient relationship. Physician Michael E. Kottow argues that any breach of patient confidentiality causes harms that are more serious than hypothetical benefits.

ISSUE 9. Is Involuntary Commitment Wrong? 148

YES: Thomas S. Szasz, from "Involuntary Mental Hospitalization: A Crime Against Humanity," *Ideology and Insanity* 150

NO: Paul Chodoff, from "The Case for Involuntary Hospitalization of the Mentally Ill," *American Journal of Psychiatry* 157

Psychiatrist Thomas S. Szasz maintains that the detention of persons in mental institutions against their will is a crime against humanity. People are not committed because they are "mentally ill" or "dangerous," but because society wants to control their behavior. Psychiatrist Paul Chodoff believes

that the rights of the mentally ill to be treated are being set aside in the rush to give them their freedom. He favors a return to the use of medical criteria by psychiatrists, albeit with legal safeguards.

ISSUE 10. Should Doctors Cut Costs at the Bedside?   **168**

YES: **Percy Brazil**, from "Cost Effective Care Is Better Care," *Hastings Center Report*   **170**

NO: **Allen R. Dyer**, from "Patients, Not Costs, Come First," *Hastings Center Report*   **174**

Physician Percy Brazil asserts that cost containment in medical care is a fact of life, and that the responsibility of the medical profession should be to ensure that the new system provides quality care. Psychiatrist Allen R. Dyer argues that the physician's primary responsibility is to the patient. To ask conscientious physicians to bear the responsibility for lowering costs creates a conflict of interest that threatens to alter the nature of the doctor-patient relationship.

ISSUE 11. Can Deception in Research Be Justified?   **182**

YES: **Stanley Milgram**, from "Subject Reaction: The Neglected Factor in the Ethics of Experimentation," *Hastings Center Report*   **184**

NO: **Diana Baumrind**, from "Research Using Intentional Deception: Ethical Issues Revisited," *American Psychologist*   **192**

The late psychologist Stanley Milgram believed that the central moral justification for allowing deceptive experiments is that the vast majority of subjects who take part in them find them acceptable after the rationale is explained. Social psychologist Diana Baumrind argues that the costs of using deception in research to subjects, the profession, and society outweigh any benefits.

ISSUE 12. Is It Ethical to Implant Animal Hearts in Humans?   **202**

YES: **Arthur L. Caplan**, from "Ethical Issues Raised by Research Involving Xenografts," *Journal of the American Medical Association*   **204**

NO: **George J. Annas**, from "Baby Fae: The 'Anything Goes' School of Human Experimentation," *Hastings Center Report*   **209**

Philosopher Arthur L. Caplan declares that since there is a serious shortage of human organs for transplantation, it is ethically defensible to allow research involving transplantation of animal hearts to proceed in those areas where no reasonable alternative therapy exists. Attorney George J. Annas

maintains that the experiment on Baby Fae did not receive adequate ethical review or appropriate consent and that it was unjustified and premature.

ISSUE 13. Should Research with Aborted Fetal Tissue Be Banned?   **216**

YES: **James Tunstead Burtchaell**, from "University Policy on Experimental Use of Aborted Fetal Tissue," *IRB: A Review of Human Subjects Research*   **218**

NO: **Benjamin Freedman**, from "The Ethics of Using Human Fetal Tissue," *IRB: A Review of Human Subjects Research*   **227**

Theologian James Tunstead Burtchaell declares that experimentation with fetal tissue is unethical because of the lack of informed consent and because it places researchers in moral complicity with abortion. Philosopher Benjamin Freedman declares that it would be wrong for the state to prohibit the use of aborted fetal tissues because there is no consensus on the moral status of the fetus and because the practice does not violate norms of consent.

ISSUE 14. Should Animal Experimentation Be Permitted?   **236**

YES: **Office of Technology Assessment**, from "Alternatives to Animal Use in Research, Testing, and Education"   **238**

NO: **Tom Regan**, from "Ill-Gotten Gains," *Health Care Ethics: An Introduction*   **248**

The Office of Technology Assessment acknowledges the conflict of interests between the use of animals for human ends, and the need of animals to be free from suffering, but concludes that when suffering inflicted on animals is unavoidable to satisfy human objectives, the human interest will be controlling. Philosopher Tom Regan argues that conducting research on animals exacts the grave moral price of failing to show proper respect for their inherent value, whatever the benefits of the research.

ISSUE 15. Should Organ Procurement Be Based on Voluntarism?   **258**

YES: **Blair L. Sadler and Alfred M. Sadler, Jr.**, from "A Community of Givers, Not Takers," *Hastings Center Report*   **260**

NO: **Charles J. Dougherty**, from "A Proposal for Ethical Organ Donation," *Health Affairs*   **267**

Physician Alfred M. Sadler, Jr., and attorney Blair Sadler maintain that the system of encouraged voluntarism increases the supply of organs without infringing on the rights of individuals and families. Philosopher Charles J. Dougherty argues that current laws should be overridden in favor of a

system of routine removal, in which physicians would retrive organs from newly-dead persons unless the next of kin refused.

ISSUE 16. Should Newborns Without Brains Be Used as Organ Donors? 272

YES: Michael R. Harrison, from "Organ Procurement for Children: The Anencephalic Fetus as Donor," *The Lancet* 274

NO: John D. Arras and Shlomo Shinnar, from "Anencephalic Newborns as Organ Donors: A Critique," *Journal of the American Medical Association* 281

Pediatric surgeon Michael R. Harrison believes that if anencephalic newborns were treated as brain-dead rather than as brain-absent, their organs could be transplanted and their families could be offered the consolation that their loss provided life for another child. Philosopher John D. Arras and pediatric neurologist Shlomo Shinnar argue that the current principles of the strict definition of brain death are sound public policy and good ethics.

ISSUE 17. Should There Be a Market in Body Parts? 288

YES: Lori B. Andrews, from "My Body, My Property," *Hastings Center Report* 290

NO: Thomas H. Murray, from "Gifts of the Body and the Needs of Strangers," *Hastings Center Report* 298

Attorney Lori B. Andrews believes that donors, recipients, and society will benefit from a market in body parts so long as owners—and no one else— retain control over their bodies. Ethicist Thomas H. Murray argues that the gift relationship should govern transfer of body parts because it honors important human values, which are diminished by market relationships.

ISSUE 18. Should Insurance Companies Be Allowed to Screen for Antibodies to the AIDS Virus? 308

YES: American Council of Life Insurance, from "White Paper: The Acquired Immunodeficiency Syndrome and HTLV-III Antibody Testing" 310

NO: Mark Scherzer, from *AIDS and the Law: A Guide for the Public* 316

The health and life insurance industries believe that their obligation to use sound underwriting practices requires the use of screening tests for antibodies to HTLV-III, the virus that causes AIDS. Attorney Mark Scherzer argues that maintaining insurance coverage for AIDS serves important social goals and that the insurance industry has exaggerated its potential losses.

ISSUE 19. Should Health Care for the Elderly Be Limited?   326

YES: Daniel Callahan, from "Limiting Health Care for the Old?" *The Nation*   328

NO: Amitai Etzioni, from "Spare the Old, Save the Young," *The Nation*   333

Philosopher Daniel Callahan believes that government has an obligation to provide those health care resources that help people live out a natural life span. Beyond that point, only the means necessary for the relief of suffering, not those for life-extending technology, should be provided. Sociologist Amitai Etzioni argues that rationing health care for the elderly would encourage conflict between generations and would invite restrictions on health care for other groups.

ISSUE 20. Is Genetic Engineering a Threat to Future Generations?   340

YES: Hans Jonas, from "Ethics and Biogenetic Art," *Social Research*   342

NO: President's Commission for the Study of Ethical Problems in Research, from *Splicing Life*   351

Philosopher Hans Jonas believes that expanding the uses of genetic engineering from bacteria to humans would open a Pandora's box of evils. We should not tamper with the inviolability of the human image. The President's Commission concludes that genetic engineering is not intrinsically wrong for humans and sees no fundamental danger to world safety or human values in any current or planned forms of the technology.

CRIME AND CRIMINOLOGY,
First Edition

ISSUE 1. Is Crime Functional?   **2**

YES: Emile Durkheim, from *Rules of Sociological Method*   **4**

NO: Jeffrey H. Reiman, from *The Rich Get Richer and the Poor Get Prison: Ideology, Class, and Criminal Justice, 2/e*   **9**

Classic sociologist Durkheim (1858–1917) theorizes that crime exists in all societies because it reaffirms moral boundaries and at times assists needed social changes. American University philosopher Jeffrey Reiman responds that crime is functional not because it promotes social solidarity but because it provides an ideology to justify the status quo.

ISSUE 2. Is Crime Created by Society's Elites?   **14**

YES: Richard Quinney, from *The Social Reality of Crime*   **16**

NO: Daniel Bell, from *The End of Ideology*   **25**

Marxist criminologist Richard Quinney theorizes that crime is largely socially constructed by society's elites to control the less powerful. Harvard sociologist Daniel Bell argues that fits of social control are more likely to be the result of middle-class moral indignation rather than policies benefiting the elite. For Bell, crime is often the ingeneous acts of members of emerging ethnic groups who seek a piece of the pie by providing services to others.

ISSUE 3. Is Criminal Behavior Biologically Determined?   **36**

YES: C. R. Jeffery, from "Criminology as an Interdisciplinary Behavioral Science," *Criminology*   **38**

NO: Tony Platt and Paul Takagi, from "Biosocial Criminology: A Critique," *Crime and Social Justice*   **45**

Florida State University criminologist C. R. Jeffery argues that physiological and chemical imbalances are frequently the precipitants of criminal behavior. Therefore, research into causes and possible cures might be better placed in the hands of medical researchers. Characterizing Jeffery's proposals as ridiculous and dangerous, *Crime and Social Justice* editors Tony Platt and Paul Takagi contend that Jeffery's ideas suffer from a poor understanding of biology, history, and criminology.

ISSUE 4. Is Street Crime More Serious Than White-Collar Crime?   52

YES: James Q. Wilson and Richard J. Herrnstein, from *Crime and Human Nature*   54

NO: Jeffrey H. Reiman from *The Rich Get Richer and the Poor Get Prison*, 2/e   65

UCLA professor James Q. Wilson and Harvard psychologist Richard J. Herrnstein argue that the focus of crime study ought to be on persons who "hit, rape, murder, steal, and threaten." American University professor Jeffrey Reiman fumes that a focus on street crimes is little more than a cover-up for more serious crimes such as pollution, medical malpractice, and dangerous working conditions that go uncorrected.

ISSUE 5. Are Official Statistics Meaningful?   84

YES: A. Keith Bottomley and Ken Pease, from *Crime and Punishment: Interpreting the Data*   86

NO: Bruce Jackson, from *Law and Disorder: Criminal Justice in America*   93

British criminologists A. Keith Bottomley and Ken Pease, while acknowledging problems with official statistics, nonetheless maintain that they are extremely useful and can be helpful for both analyzing crime and generating a more humane criminal justice system. Social critic Bruce Jackson disagrees, claiming that official statistics are virtually worthless for understanding the types, rates, or distributions of crime.

ISSUE 6. Is Crime Getting Worse?   102

YES: Elliott Currie, from *Confronting Crime: An American Challenge*   104

NO: Kevin N. Wright, from *The Great American Crime Myth*   109

University of California criminal justice researcher Elliott Currie compares the rates of crimes of violence in the United States with other industrial nations and concludes that both the reality and threat of crime are escalating. State University of New York criminal justice administration professor Kevin N. Wright counters that the so-called crime wave is a creation of the mass media and that the claim of an increasing rate of crime is a major myth of criminology.

ISSUE 7. Has the Women's Movement Increased Female Criminality?   118

YES: Freda Adler, from *Sisters in Crime*   120

NO: Darrell J. Steffensmeier, from "Trends in Female Crime: It's Still a Man's World," *USA Today Magazine* (a publication of the Society for the Advancement of Education)   126

Sociologist Freda Adler contends that women's liberation has caused the "feminization" of crime, and she asserts that female crime rates have increased at a far greater rate than those of males. Pennsylvania State University criminologist D. J. Steffensmeier disagrees with Adler's liberation thesis. He re-analyzes Adler's data and insists that, if anything, female crime trends have remained the same or even decreased.

ISSUE 8. Is the Criminal Justice System Racist?   140

YES: Anthony G. Amsterdam, from "Race and the Death Penalty," *Criminal Justice Ethics*   142

NO: William Wilbanks, from *The Myth of a Racist Criminal Justice System*   149

New York University Law School professor Anthony G. Amsterdam, drawing from his own work on capital punishment in Georgia as well as several massive studies dealing with the fairness of capital sentencing in that state, concludes that gross violations of ethics and law occur there and elsewhere in the United States as a result of racism. Florida International University criminologist William Wilbanks raises several important issues in his defense of the criminal justice system, especially against charges of racism in sentencing. While acknowledging that there are racist police officers, district attorneys, and judges, he contends that, overall, criminal justice is fair.

ISSUE 9. Should the Police Direct Community Crime Prevention?   156

YES: Douglas E. Rake, from "Crime Control and Police-Community Relations: A Cross-Cultural Comparison," *Annals of the American Academy of Political and Social Science*   158

NO: Ronald L. Boostrom and Joel H. Henderson, from "The Ideology of Community Crime Prevention," *Journal of Security Administration*   165

Telecommunications expert Douglas E. Rake compares community-police relations in two cities and maintains that citizen willingness to cooperate with the police contributes to these two cities' relatively low crime rates. San Diego State University professors of criminal justice administration Ron Boostrom and Joel Henderson register serious concerns about increasing police involvement within neighborhoods. They warn that the possibility of expanding police power may be little more than a way to cover up police and other policy failures.

ISSUE 10. Juvenile Justice: Are Kids "Getting Away With Murder"? 172

YES: Alfred S. Regnery, from "Getting Away with Murder: Why the Juvenile Justice System Needs an Overhaul," *Policy Review*   174

NO: Stephen J. Brodt and J. Steven Smith, from "Public Policy and the Serious Juvenile Offender," *Criminal Justice Policy Review*   181

Office of Juvenile Justice and Delinquency Prevention administrator Alfred S. Regnery says that children commit one-third of all crimes yet are not held accountable for their acts. He calls for a return to the doctrine of deterrence since the old rehabilitation philosophy has clearly failed. Ball State University criminologists Stephen J. Brodt and J. Steven Smith reject Regnery's view of juvenile delinquency as well as the solutions he proposes. The authors make their case and assert that claims that juveniles are getting away with murder are greatly exaggerated and that rehabilitation remains a workable ideal.

ISSUE 11. Should Lawyers Use "Hardball" Tactics?   192

YES: Stephanie B. Goldberg, from "Playing Hardball," *American Bar Association Journal*   194

NO: Robert N. Sayler, from "Rambo Litigation: Why Hardball Tactics Don't Work," *American Bar Association Journal*   200

American Bar Association Journal assistant editor Stephanie B. Goldberg polls several lawyers about their perceptions and opinions of "hardball" legal tactics and concludes that justice is sometimes served if attorneys use such tactics to win cases for their clients. Washington, D. C. attorney Robert N. Sayler, in a biting dismissal of the claims made for hardball tactics, contends that they are bad for clients, for the lawyers who use them, and for the legal profession itself.

ISSUE 12. Is Selective Incapacitation Just?   206

YES: Brian Forst, from "Selective Incapacitation: A Sheep in Wolf's Clothing?" *Judicature*   208

NO: Andrew von Hirsch, from "Selective Incapacitation Reexamined," *Criminal Justice Ethics*   216

Brian Forst, director of research for INSLAW, Inc., says that we now have the capacity to identify repeat offenders who pose a threat to society. So why not give them longer sentences, which will keep them off the streets and significantly reduce crime? Professor of criminal justice Andrew von Hirsch dismisses Forst's ideas and argues that we do not have the ability to identify such criminals, nor would it be just to give them longer sentences even if we knew for certain who they were.

ISSUE 13. Should Capital Punishment Be Abolished?   226

YES: Jack Greenberg, from "Against the American System of Capital
Punishment," *Harvard Law Review*   228

NO: Ernest van den Haag, from "The Ultimate Punishment: A
Defense," *Harvard Law Review*   232

Columbia Law School professor Jack Greenberg maintains that capital
punishment is unfairly administered and ineffective, both as a deterrent and
as a punishment. Fordham University professor Ernest van den Haag
challenges those who claim that capital punishment is barbaric and unfair.
He insists that capital punishment does deter criminals and is just retribution
for terrible crimes.

ISSUE 14. Do We Need More Jails?   242

YES: Dale A. Nederhoff, from "Crowding Crunch in County Jails
Demands Fast Track Concept," *Corrections Today*   244

NO: John Irwin, from *The Jail: Managing the Underclass in American
Society*   248

Planner Dale A. Nederhoff proposes that the rapid and efficient expansion of
jails will solve the jail crowding problem. San Francisco State University
sociologist and former prison inmate John Irwin pleads for an examination of
our existing values, not more jails, in order to find ways of helping jail
inmates, who he views as victims of overzealous members of the criminal
justice system.

ISSUE 15. Will Gun Control Reduce Crime?   254

YES: Josh Sugarmann, from "The NRA Is Right: But We Still Need to
Ban Handguns," *Washington Monthly*   256

NO: James D. Wright, from "Second Thoughts About Gun Control,"
Public Interest   262

Josh Sugarmann, formerly with the National Coalition to Ban Handguns,
identifies several problems with legalized handguns, including what he
describes as unacceptably high rates of suicides with guns, family homicides,
and accidents. Massachusetts Institute of Technology sociologist James D.
Wright argues that banning small handguns would not reduce crime. He
also sets forth what he classifies as the many legitimate uses of Saturday
night specials.

ISSUE 16. Should We Send Convicts to Penal Colonies?   272

YES: Tom Murton, from "Back to the Future: An Alternative to the Prison Dilemma," *Paper presented at the Western Society of Criminology*   274

NO: Alexander E. Hooke, from "Convicts, Deviants, and Flawed Utopias," *Paper presented at the Western Society of Criminology*   282

Visiting professor of sociology at the University of Hawaii Tom Murton contends that penal colonies can be both just and practical. Villa Julie College philosopher Alex Hooke is amused by Murton's proposal but raises questions about both its ethics and practicality.

ISSUE 17. Will Drug Legalization Help the Criminal Justice System? 290

YES: Arnold S. Trebach, from "*Law Enforcement News* Interview with Trebach," *Law Enforcement News*   292

NO: John Kaplan, from "Taking Drugs Seriously," *Public Interest*   299

American University School of Justice professor Arnold S. Trebach pulls no punches by insisting that the war against illegal drugs is lost. Thus, he says, the only sensible path remaining is to immediately make many drugs legal. John Kaplan, from Stanford Law School, counters that legalization is not the answer. The lesser evil, he feels, is to step up our fight against hard-core drug use and sales in order to reduce crime.

ISSUE 18. Is the Victims' Rights Movement Succeeding?   308

YES: Marlene A. Young, from "*Law Enforcement News* Interview with Young," *Law Enforcement News*   310

NO: Robert Elias, from *The Politics of Victimization: Victims, Victimology, and Human Rights*   320

Marlene A. Young, executive director of the National Organizations for Victim Assistance, supports the existing system for helping victims. Drawing from her own work, she calls for more funding and services within the current structures. Political scientist Robert Elias contends that the victim's movement has hurt both victims and defendants while helping only certain aspects of the criminal justice system.

ECONOMIC ISSUES,
Fourth Edition

ISSUE 1. Are Profits the Only Business of Business?   **2**

Yes: Milton Friedman, from "The Social Responsibility of Business Is to Increase Its Profits," *New York Times Magazine*   **4**

No: Robert Almeder, from "The Ethics of Profits: Reflections on Corporate Responsibility," *Business and Society*   **10**

Free market economist Milton Friedman contends that the sole responsibility of business is to increase its profits. Philosopher Robert Almeder maintains that if capitalism is to survive, it must act in socially responsible ways that go beyond profit making.

ISSUE 2. Should We Try to Save the Family Farm?   **20**

Yes: Byron Dorgan, from "America's Real Farm Problem: It Can Be Solved," *The Washington Monthly*   **22**

No: Stephan Chapman, from "The Farmer on the Dole," *Harper's*   **32**

Representative Dorgan of North Dakota fears that public policy has become too concerned with the interests of the large corporate farms while ignoring the small family farm that has "made agriculture one of the few American industries still competitive in international markets." Columnist Chapman argues for "rugged individualism." He asserts that: "If Americans still believe in the virtue of hardy rural self-reliance, they should tell Washington to get out of the way and let farmers practice it."

ISSUE 3. Should We Create More Competition in the Blood-Banking Industry?   **40**

Yes: Ross D. Eckert, from "AIDS and the Blood Bankers," *Regulation*   **42**

No: Joseph R. Bove, M.D., from "Directed Donations," *Legal Issues in Transfusion Medicine*   **54**

Economist Eckert maintains that the problem with the blood banking industry is that "increased regulation" has led to "a basically noncompetitive environment that is inferior to a competitively organized blood market." Physician and Professor of Laboratory Medicine Bove argues that "directed donor programs" might "jeopardize the national blood supply."

ISSUE 4. Is "Comparable Worth" Worthless?   62

Yes: Clifford Hackett, from "Woman, Work, and the Question of 'Comparable Worth': Better from a Distance," *Commonweal*   64

No: Ruth Needleman, from "Pay Equity: Freeing the Market from Discrimination," *original essay for this volume*   70

Social critic Hackett argues that comparable worth would put an end to the "laws of supply and demand or other economic principles that determine wage rates for different kinds of work." Labor economist Needleman contends that pay differentials between men and women cannot be traced to differentials in "human capital." She concludes that these differentials result from discriminatory practices and attitudes.

ISSUE 5. Are There Too Many Hostile Takeovers?   78

Yes: Gerald L. Houseman, from "The Merger Game Starts with Deception," *Challenge*   80

No: John D. Paulus and Robert S. Gay, from "U.S. Mergers Are Helping Productivity," *Challenge*   87

Political science professor Houseman asserts that the economic rewards reaped by Wall Street takeover artists come at the expense of workers, stockholders, and the general public. Business economists Paulus and Gay argue that the corporate restructuring of the 1980s is a direct result of the need to increase productivity in the face of declining U.S. competitiveness.

ISSUE 6. Should the Federal Government Deregulate American Business?   96

Yes: Murray L. Weidenbaum, from "Weidenbaum Analyzes Benefit-Cost Analysis," *Across the Board*   98

No: The editors of Dollars and Sense, from "OSHA Hits Brown Lung Rules," *Dollars and Sense*   104

Weidenbaum asserts that government decision makers should face the same economic constraints as business executives do in the private sector. They must insist that the benefit of their actions at least match the cost of their actions. The editors of *Dollars and Sense* contend that although benefit-cost analysis seems to have a "certain simple logic," it is neither simple nor objective. Rather, they believe benefit-cost analysis and the related cost- effectiveness approach are fatally flawed by an inherent social bias.

ISSUE 7. Do Firms Exploit Workers and Local Communities by Closing Profitable Plants? 110

Yes: Barry Bluestone and Bennett Harrison, from "Why Corporations Close Profitable Plants," *Working Papers* 112

No: Richard B. McKenzie, from "Frustrating Business Mobility," *Regulation* 122

Professors Bluestone and Harrison assert that large modern corporations (particularly conglomerates) systematically milk profits from healthy firms, mismanage them, fail to maintain them, and then shut them down on the grounds that they are inefficient. Professor McKenzie argues that in a healthy market economy it is natural and necessary for some firms to move and others to close in order to achieve the benefits of economic efficiency.

ISSUE 8. Should Congress Guarantee U.S. Workers the Right to Parental Leave? 132

Yes: from "Background and Need for Legislation," *Parental and Medical Leave Act of 1986* 134

No: from "Separate Dissenting Views on H.R. 4300, The Family and Medical Leave Act of 1986," *Parental and Medical Leave Act of 1986* 141

Supporters of H.R. 4300 maintain that there is a "growing conflict between work and family" that can be corrected by guaranteeing workers the "right to unpaid family leave." The dissenting members of the House Committee on Education and Labor argue that H.R. 4300 may be "well-intentioned," but it is also "rigid and inflexible."

ISSUE 9. Is It Time to Abolish the Minimum Wage? 148

Yes: The editors of *The Nation's Business*, from "Minimum Wage Myths," *The Nation's Business* 150

No: Teresa Ghilarducci, from "Women's Jobs and the Minimum Wage," *testimony prepared for the Pennsylvania House of Representatives* 155

The editors of *The Nation's Business* insist that support for the minimum wage is based on eight myths that ignore the fact that if the Kennedy-Hawkins bill passes, it "hurts the very employees it is intended to help." Economist Ghilarducci maintains that both "advocates and detractors of the minimum wage" have ignored the impact it has had on the economic well-being of "women workers."

ISSUE 10. Has American Government Become Too Big?   166

Yes: William Simon, from "The Road to Liberty," *A Time For Truth*   168

No: John Kenneth Galbraith, from "The Social Consensus and the Conservative Onslaught," *Millenium Journal of International Studies*   174

Former Treasury Secretary Simon argues that government has gone too far in its efforts to provide "cradle-to-grave security." According to Simon, wealth can only be created through the free operation of markets, and it is imperative that productivity and the growth of productivity be given the highest economic priority. Harvard economist Galbraith believes that the services provided by government contribute as much to the well-being of society as those provided by the private sector. Although taxes may reduce the freedom of those who are taxed, the freedom of those who benefit from the tax-financed programs is enhanced.

ISSUE 11. Can Monetary and Fiscal Policies Still Be Used to Solve Our Macroeconomic Problems?   180

Yes: Walter W. Heller, from "Activist Government: Key to Growth," *Challenge*   182

No: Marc Levinson, from "Economic Policy: The Old Tools Won't Work," *Dun's Business Month*   189

Economist Heller argues that history demonstrates that an activist government can improve macroeconomic performance. Heller believes that a return to activist government with proper alignment and execution of monetary and fiscal policies would solve problems in poverty and productivity. Journalist Levinson believes that the economic environment has changed. The internationalization of the U.S. economy means that "even the greatest of economic powers can no longer control its own destiny."

ISSUE 12. Is Tax Reform an Impossible Dream Come True?   196

Yes: Henry J. Aaron, from "The Impossible Dream Comes True: The New Tax Reform Act," *The Brookings Review*   198

No: Henning Gutmann, from "The Bad New Tax Law," *New York Review of Books*   206

Economist Aaron believes that the Tax Reform Act of 1986 represents "a major tax overhaul that deserves to be honored as reform." Although the new tax legislation can be criticized for certain things, Aaron argues that it has made the tax system "more conducive to economic efficiency and

growth, fairer, and simpler." Reporter Gutmann sees a number of problems with the Tax Reform Act, and believes it is "a clear step backward for the progressive idea of taxation."

ISSUE 13. Is the Welfare System Causing Poverty? 214

Yes: Charles Murray, from "Welfare: Promoting Poverty or Progress," *The Wall Street Journal* 216

No: Richard D. Coe and Greg J. Duncan, from "Welfare: Promoting Poverty or Progress," *The Wall Street Journal* 220

Researcher Murray believes that the welfare reforms of the 1960s and the changes in the ways government treated the poor caused low income youth to "become decoupled from the mechanism whereby poor people in this country historically have worked their way out of poverty." College professor Coe and researcher Duncan argue that "typical welfare spells are brief, interspersed with work, do not break up families, and are not passed on from parent to child."

ISSUE 14. Can Federal Budget Deficits Be Good for the Economy? 224

Yes: Robert Eisner, from "Will the Real Federal Deficit Stand Up?" *Challenge* 226

No: Paul Wonnacott, from "The Nominal Deficit Really Matters," *Challenge* 235

Economist Eisner believes that to correctly measure the impact of the deficit on the economy, the budget figures must be adjusted for changes in output or employment and inflation. His analysis also suggests that an effort to achieve a conventionally measured balanced budget would cause a severe recession. Professor Paul Wonnacott, an economist at the University of Maryland, also discusses the need to adjust the budget deficit for the level of unemployment. But he rejects the idea of further adjustments for inflation, and he concludes that it may not be completely necessary to eliminate the current deficit completely.

ISSUE 15. Did Monetary Policy Cause the Stock Market Crash in 1987? 242

Yes: Paul Craig Roberts, from ". . . Too Tight Already," *The Wall Street Journal* 244

No: James K. Glassman, from "Where Did It All Go?" *The New Republic* 247

Economist Roberts believes that the stock market crash was caused by the tight monetary policy of the Federal Reserve System. Glassman argues

that the crash represented a return to more realistic, more reasonable stock prices because in October 1987 the market was overvalued.

ISSUE 16. Should the U. S. Protect Domestic Industries from Foreign Competition? 254

Yes: Bob Kuttner, from "The Free Trade Fallacy," *The New Republic* 256

No: Michael Kinsley, from "Keep Free Trade Free," *The New Republic* 263

Columnist Kuttner writes that "comparative advantage" is determined by exploitative wage rates and government action; it is not determined by free markets. Social critic Kinsley replies that we do not decrease American living standards when we import the products made by cheap foreign labor. He claims protectionism today, just as it did in the eighteenth century, weakens our economy and only "helps to put off the day of reckoning."

ISSUE 17. Will the Third World Pay Its Debt? 268

Yes: Gary Hector, from "Third World Debt: The Bomb Is Defused," *Fortune* 270

No: Alfred Watkins, from "Going For Broke?" *Report on the Americas* 276

Business journalist Hector argues that the danger of an international financial calamity "now appears remote." Economist Watkins suggests that a "rather simple benefit-cost analysis" indicates that "default may be the most viable and profitable option" for the debtor nations.

ISSUE 18. Is the Pain and Suffering Associated with Disinvestment and Sanctions Worth It for Black South African Workers? 290

Yes: David T. Beaty and Oren Harari, from "South Africa: White Manager, Black Voices," *Harvard Business Review* 292

No: Helen Suzman, from "The Folly of Economic Sanctions," *Business and Society Review* 301

Management experts Beaty and Harari argue that whether or not disinvestment will hurt black workers must be examined in light of the belief of many blacks that "investment hasn't helped them in the first place." Helen Suzman, a long- time member of the Progressive Federal Party in the South African Parliament, argues that economic sanctions will ruin the South African economy for all.

ISSUE 19. Is the Middle Class Shrinking? 310

Yes: Katharine L. Bradbury, from "The Shrinking Middle Class," *New England Economic Review* 312

No: Frank Levy, from "The Middle Class: Is It Really Vanishing?" *The Brookings Review* 322

Katharine L. Bradbury, an economist formerly with the Federal Reserve Bank of Boston, believes that the middle class is shrinking; that is, there was a decline in the percentage of families with middle class incomes between 1973 and 1984. Frank Levy, an economist at the University of Maryland, sees substantial stability in the distribution of income over time.

ISSUE 20. Is Manufacturing Alive and Well and Living in the U.S.? 328

Yes: Molly McUsic, from "U.S. Manufacturing: Any Cause for Alarm?" *New England Economic Review* 330

No: Nicholas S. Perna, from "The Shift from Manufacturing to Services: A Concerned View," *New England Economic Review* 340

McUsic, a former researcher at the Federal Reserve Bank of Boston, examines the behavior of output, employment, and productivity in U.S. manufacturing and finds that manufacturing has maintained its relative share in U.S. total production. Perna, an economist with General Electric, is pessimistic about recent changes in the structure of the economy and identifies several symptoms of ill health in manufacturing.

EDUCATIONAL ISSUES,
Fifth Edition

ISSUE 1. Should Schooling Be Based on Students' Social Experiences? 2
YES: John Dewey, from *Experience and Education*   **4**
NO: Robert M. Hutchins, from *The Conflict in Education*   **12**

John Dewey suggests a reconsideration of traditional approaches to schooling, giving fuller attention to the social development of the learner and the quality of his total experience. Robert M. Hutchins argues for a liberal arts education geared to the development of intellectual powers.

ISSUE 2. Should Schools Determine What Is Learned?   **18**
YES: Clifton Fadiman, from *The Case for Basic Education*   **20**
NO: John Holt, from *Escape from Childhood*   **27**

Clifton Fadiman argues for standardized subject matter, which rescues the learner from triviality and capriciousness. John Holt feels that an imposed curriculum damages the individual and usurps a basic human right to select one's own path of development.

ISSUE 3. Should Curricula Emphasize Commonality Over Diversity?   **34**
YES: Richard Rodriquez, from "What Is an American Education?"
The Los Angeles Times   **36**
NO: Alba A. Rosenman, from "The Value of Multicultural Curricula,"
Education Week   **40**

Richard Rodriguez presents the case that the United States, as a society of immigrants, must be bound together by knowledge of the dominant cultural heritage. Alba Rosenman counters with an anti-assimilationist argument for augmenting cultural diversity.

ISSUE 4. Should Values Be Developed Rather Than Transmitted?   **44**
YES: Lawrence Kohlberg, from "The Cognitive-Developmental
Approach to Moral Education," *Phi Delta Kappan*   **46**
NO: Edward A. Wynne, from "The Great Tradition in Education:
Transmitting Moral Values," *Educational Leadership*   **55**

Lawrence Kohlberg outlines his theory which, following Dewey and Piaget, links values to cognitive growth. Edward Wynne feels that the schools, under the influence of Kohlberg and others, have abandoned our educational traditions.

ISSUE 5. Is Church-State Separation Being Threatened?   64

YES: R. Freeman Butts, from "A History and Civics Lesson for Us All," *Educational Leadership*   66

NO: Robert L. Cord, from "Church-State Separation and the Public Schools: A Re-evaluation," *Educational Leadership*   72

R. Freeman Butts warns that current efforts to redefine the relationship between religion and schooling erode the Constitution's intent. Robert Cord offers a different interpretation of this intent, one which is more accommodating.

ISSUE 6. Does Behavioral Control Provide the Best Learning Environment?   82

YES: B. F. Skinner, from *Beyond Freedom and Dignity*   84

NO: Carl Rogers, from *Freedom to Learn*   90

B. F. Skinner offers a critique of the concept of "inner freedom" and links learning and motivation to the influence of external forces. Carl Rogers offers the "humanistic" alternative to behaviorism, insisting on the reality of subjective forces in human motivation.

ISSUE 7. Should Compulsory Schooling Be Abolished?   98

YES: Ivan Illich, from *Deschooling Society*   100

NO: Philip Jackson, from "Deschooling? NO!" *Today's Education*   107

Ivan Illich calls for replacing government-compelled schooling with community-based skill and knowledge exchanges open to all. Philip Jackson finds faulty premises and a good deal of illogic in Illich's position and recommends internal school reforms.

ISSUE 8. Should Schools Serve National Economic Needs?   116

YES: James B. Hunt, Jr., from Education for Economic Growth: A Critical Investment *Phi Delta Kappan*   118

NO: Joel Spring, from "Education and the Sony War," *Phi Delta Kappan*   **126**

James B. Hunt, Jr., former governor of North Carolina, argues that students must learn the skills that are necessary for the improvement of the American economy. Joel Spring counters with the contentions the the schools are becoming increasingly captive to the profit-motive of business and industry.

ISSUE 9. Are the Cards Stacked Against True School Reform?   **134**

YES: John I. Goodlad, from "A Study of Schooling: Some Findings and Hypotheses," *Phi Delta Kappan*   **136**

NO: Amitai Etzioni, from "Education for Mutuality and Civility," *The Futurist*   **148**

John Goodlad summarizes his extensive research, uncovering a set of factors that contribute to curricular and methodological inertia. Amitai Etzioni finds hope for the reconstruction of schooling in current ideas and efforts to restore "psychic stamina" through character formation.

ISSUE 10. Must All Students Be Given the Same Kind of Schooling? 156

YES: Mortimer J. Adler, from "The Paideia Proposal: Rediscovering the Essence of Education," *American School Board Journal*   **158**

NO: Floretta Dukes McKenzie, from "The Yellow Brick Road of Education," *Harvard Educational Review*   **165**

Mortimer Adler contends that equality of educational opportunity can be attained in qualitative terms by establishing uniform curricular objectives for all. Floretta Dukes McKenzie points out Adler's faulty assumptions about the learning process and his lack of attention to the realities of contemporary society.

ISSUE 11. Are Proposed Elementary School Reforms Realistic?   **172**

YES: William J. Bennett, from "First Lessons," *Phi Delta Kappan*   **174**

NO: Albert Shanker, from "A Mixed Bag," *Phi Delta Kappan*   **183**

Former secretary of education William Bennett contends that the keys to the improvement of elementary education lie in inventive leadership, a strengthened parental role, and an explicit curriculum. Teachers' union president Albert Shanker finds Bennett's report long on value judgments and short on the clear identification of ways to accomplish the desired goals.

ISSUE 12. Should Very Young Children Receive Academic Instruction?   188

YES: Siegfried and Therese Engelmann, from *Give Your Child a Superior Mind*   190

NO: David Elkind, from "Formal Education and Early Childhood Education: An Essential Difference," *Phi Delta Kappan*   197

The Engelmanns, as advocates of teaching academic skills to preschool children, offer a program through which parents can shape the learning environment. David Elkind, a leading critic of "superkid" programs, insists that formal instruction does not fit the preschooler's unique modes of learning.

ISSUE 13. Are Specific Programs to Teach Thinking Needed?   208

YES: Jay McTighe, from "Teaching for Thinking, of Thinking, and About Thinking," *School*   210

NO: Mortimer J. Adler, from "Why 'Critical Thinking' Programs Won't Work," *Education Week*   216

Jay McTighe argues that adding new, direct approaches to our usual efforts to teach thinking is necessary. Mortimer Adler feels that getting students to think about what is being taught would suffice.

ISSUE 14. Should Literacy Be Based on Traditional Culture?   220

YES: E. D. Hirsch, Jr., from "Restoring Cultural Literacy in Early Grades," *Educational Leadership*   222

NO: Stephen Tchudi, from "Slogans Indeed: A Reply to Hirsch," *Educational Leadership*   232

E. D. Hirsch argues that educators need to re-examine slogans that undermine the teaching of traditional knowledge to young children. Stephen Tchudi contends that cultural literacy cannot be prescribed, since it evolves from the complexities of children's experience.

ISSUE 15. Is Measurement-Driven Instruction Desirable?   238

YES: W. James Popham, from "The Merits of Measurement-Driven Instruction," *Phi Delta Kappan*   240

NO: Gerald W. Bracey, from "Measurement-Driven Instruction: Catchy Phrase, Dangerous Practice" *Phi Delta Kappan*   247

W. James Popham protrays measurement-driven instruction as the most cost-effective way to improve the quality of public education. Gerald W. Bracey sees fragmentation, trivialization, and curricular narrowing as the true costs of this methodological approach.

ISSUE 16. Are Packaged Discipline Programs Harmful?   256

YES: Richard L. Curwin and Allen N. Mendler, from "Packaged Discipline Programs: Let the Buyer Beware," *Educational Leadership*   258

NO: Lee Canter, from "Let the Educator Beware: A Response to Curwin and Mendler," *Educational Leadership*   264

Richard Curwin and Allen Mendler argue that packaged discipline approaches obtain quick results at the expense of developing student understanding of responsibility. Lee Canter contends that his and others' programs give teachers effective strategies that lead to positive learning experiences.

ISSUE 17. Is Mainstreaming Beneficial to All?   270

YES: Dean C. Corrigan, from "Political and Moral Contexts That Produced Public Law 94-142," *Journal of Teacher Education*   272

NO: W. N. Bender, from "The Case Against Mainstreaming: Empirical Support for the Political Backlash," *Education*   278

Dean Corrigan traces the political and moral roots of Public Law 94-142 and concludes that mainstreaming can restore a sense of social purpose to the educational system. W. N. Bender reviews research evidence that shows negative effects on non-handicapped students and disruptions of the classroom ecology.

ISSUE 18. Does Tracking Support Educational Inequality?   288

YES: Jeannie Oakes, from "Keeping Track, Part 1: The Policy and Practice of Curriculum Inequality," *Phi Delta Kappan*   290

NO: Charles Nevi, from "In Defense of Tracking," *Educational Leadership*   300

Jeannie Oakes argues that tracking exaggerates initial differences among students and contributes to mediocre schooling for many who are placed in middle or lower tracks. Charles Nevi feels that tracking accommodates individual differences while making "high status knowledge" available to all.

ISSUE 19. Is Bilingual Education Justifiably As a Policy? 306

YES: Tony Baez, Ricardo Fernandez, Richard Navarro, and Roger L. Rice, from "Litigation Strategies for Educational Equity: Bilingual Education and Research," *Issues in Education* 308

NO: Diane Ravitch, from "Politicization and the Schools: The Case of Bilingual Education," *American Philosophical Society Proceedings* 321

Baez, Fernandez, Navarro, and Rice cite equity gains through litigation and call for greater cooperation between researchers and advocates. Diane Ravitch feels that research on bilingual education is inconclusive and is often misinterpreted by zealots.

ISSUE 20. Are Tests of Teacher Knowledge Fair? 332

YES: Gregory R. Anrig, from "Teacher Education and Teacher Testing: The Rush to Mandate," *Phi Delta Kappan* 334

NO: Linda Darling-Hammond, from "Teaching Knowledge: How Do We Test It?" *American Educator* 342

Gregory Anrig, president of the Educational Testing Service, makes the case for the National Teacher Examination as a legitimate tool for measuring qualifications. Linda Darling-Hammond provides examples of what she feels are serious deficiencies in this type of test.

ENVIRONMENTAL ISSUES,
Third Edition

ISSUE 1. Does Wilderness Have Intrinsic Value?   2

YES: Wilbur F. LaPage and Sally Ranney, from "The Heart and Soul
of Culture," *Parks & Recreation*   4

NO: William Tucker, from "Is Nature Too Good for Us?" *Harper's*   11

Parks administrator Wilbur LaPage and wilderness organization president
Sally Ranney contend that America's wild country shaped our national
attitudes and profoundly influences our writers, artists, and musicians.
Tucker, a writer and social critic, asserts that wilderness areas are elitist
preserves designed to keep people out.

**ISSUE 2. Do We Need More Stringently Enforced Regulations to Pro-
tect Endangered Species?**   24

YES: Lewis Regenstein, from "Endangered Species and Human
Survival," *USA Today*, a publication of the Society for the Advancement
of Education   26

NO: Richard Starnes, from "The Sham of Endangered Species," *Outdoor Life*   32

Environmentalist Regenstein charges that the policy of exploiting rather than
protecting wildlife, which was the policy of the Reagan administration,
threatens to accelerate the disappearance of endangered plant and animal
species. *Outdoor Life* editor Starnes counters that wildlife management policy
should be left to the judgment of professionals in the state and national
agencies responsible for carrying out the policies, not to the whims of federal
legislators.

**ISSUE 3. Is EPA's Strategy Evolving to Meet Present and Future
Environmental Problems?**   40

YES: Jack Lewis, from "Looking Backward: A Historical Perspective on
Environmental Regulations," *EPA Journal*   42

NO: Daniel Grossman, from "The Strategy of the Cork," *The Amicus
Journal*   47

Environmental journal editor Jack Lewis reviews the history of regulation
and suggests that EPA scientists and managers have the tools, dedication,

and ingenuity to deal with present and future challenges. Science writer Daniel Grossman raises serious questions about the inadequacies of the regulatory methods and abilities of the EPA.

ISSUE 4. Does Risk-Benefit Analysis Provide an Objective Method for Making Environmental Decisions? 52

YES: William D. Ruckelshaus, from "Science, Risk and Public Policy," *Science* 54

NO: Langdon Winner, from "Risk—Another Name for Danger," *Science for the People* 60

Former EPA administrator Ruckelshaus advocates educating the public about risk estimates and separating the scientific process of risk assessment from the management of risks through regulation. Social scientist Winner asserts that dealing with environmental and health hazards in terms of risk assessment leads to delays and confusion in efforts to regulate pollution and protect the public.

ISSUE 5. Are Environmentalists and Industrial Leaders Becoming Less Adversarial? 70

YES: Kent Gilbreath, from "Industry's Environmental Attitudes," *EPA Journal* 72

NO: G. M. Keller, from "Industry and the Environment," *Vital Speeches of the Day* 77

Business school dean Kent Gilbreath sees the dogmatism that previously characterized the debates among business leaders, environmental activists, and government regulators as giving way to a more hopeful and pragmatic spirit of cooperation. Chevron executive G. M. Keller views the dialogue on environmental issues as a deteriorating one, with increased acrimony and less trust by the public of both industrialists and government regulators.

ISSUE 6. Is Population Control the Key to Preventing Environmental Deterioration? 86

YES: Paul R. Ehrlich and John Holdren, from "Impact of Population Growth," *Science* 88

NO: Barry Commoner, Michael Corr, and Paul J. Stamler, from "The Causes of Pollution," *Environment* 96

Environmental scientists Ehrlich and Holdren argue that population increase is the principal cause of environmental degradation. Environmental scien-

tists Commoner, Corr, and Stamler contend that technological change rather than population growth has been the chief cause of environmental stress.

ISSUE 7. **Should Regulation of Airborne Toxins Under the Clean Air Act Be Strengthened?** 112

YES: **Richard E. Ayres,** from Testimony before the Subcommittee on Environmental Protection, U.S. Senate 114

NO: **Janie A. Kinney,** from Comments of Merck & Co. to the Subcommittee on Environmental Protection, U.S. Senate 121

Environmental leader Richard Ayres argues that strong, comprehensive legislation is needed to regulate toxic air emissions and accidental releases of toxins. Corporation counsel Janie Kinney presents the Merck & Co. argument that stringent controls on emissions are not justified by demonstrated adverse health effects and would constitute an inappropriate intrusion into the operations of manufacturing facilities.

ISSUE 8. **Is Nuclear Power Safe and Desirable?** 126

YES: **Alvin M. Weinberg,** from "Is Nuclear Energy Necessary?" *Bulletin of the Atomic Scientists* 128

NO: **Denis Hayes,** from "Nuclear Power: The Fifth Horseman," *World • Watch* 136

Nuclear physicist Alvin Weinberg argues that development of nuclear breeder reactors is needed to assure future energy supplies and that safety can be provided through technical improvements and siting in remote areas. Energy analyst Denis Hayes contends that developing nuclear power assures nuclear weapons proliferation and that environmentally safer energy sources are technically and economically feasible.

ISSUE 9. **Is the Widespread Use of Pesticides Required to Feed the World's People?** 144

YES: **William R. Furtick,** from "Uncontrolled Pests or Adequate Food," *Pesticides and Human Welfare* 146

NO: **Michael Dover,** from "Getting Off the Pesticide Treadmill," *Technology Review* 154

Crop protection specialist William Furtick warns that pesticides are essential for the intensive agriculture required to prevent mass starvation. Ecologist Michael Dover counters that dependence on pesticides creates serious health and environmental problems and has frequently worsened pest infestation.

ISSUE 10. Is There a Cancer Epidemic Due to Industrial Chemicals in the Environment?   164

YES: **Samuel S. Epstein,** from "Losing the War Against Cancer," *The Ecologist*   166

NO: **Elizabeth M. Whelan,** from "The Charge of the Cancer Brigade," *National Review*   176

Physician Samuel Epstein claims that preventable environmental exposure is responsible for dramatically rising human cancer rates. Physician Elizabeth Whelan asserts that the claim that we are experiencing an environmentally-caused cancer epidemic is a misconception.

ISSUE 11. Is Immediate Legislative Action Needed to Combat the Effects of Acid Rain?   184

YES: **Jon R. Luoma,** from "Acid Murder No Longer a Mystery," *Audubon*   186

NO: **A. Denny Ellerman,** from Testimony before the Subcommittee on Environmental Protection, U.S. Senate   193

Science writer Jon Luoma argues that research has produced convincing evidence that legislation requiring large cutbacks in acid gas emission is urgently needed to prevent continued destruction of forest and lake ecosystems. Coal association executive Denny Ellerman argues that sulfur oxide emissions are presently declining and further restrictions would produce marginal benefits at great cost to industry and the public.

ISSUE 12. Should Women Be Excluded from Jobs That Could Be Hazardous to a Fetus?   198

YES: **Hugh M. Finneran,** from "Title VII and Restrictions on Employment of Fertile Women," *Labor Law Journal*   200

NO: **Carolyn Marshall,** from "Fetal Protection Policies—An Excuse for Workplace Hazard," *The Nation*   208

Corporate counsel Hugh M. Finneran believes women should be excluded from occupations that threaten the unborn for humanitarian reasons as well as to protect employers from future liability. Health writer Carolyn Marshall counters that reproductive toxins are hazardous to men as well as women and that cleaning up the workplace is the only acceptable response to conditions that threaten the fetus.

ISSUE 13. Hazardous Waste: Can Present Regulatory and Voluntary
Efforts Solve Disposal and Clean-up Problems?   216

YES: David J. Hanson, from "Clean Sites, Inc., Moves Into Full Swing
With Waste Cleanup," *Chemical & Engineering News*   218

NO: Julie L. Edelson, from "Superfund Still in the Dumps," *Technology
Review*   223

Science magazine writer David Hanson reports on a private venture that is
working with government, industry, and community leaders to clean up
many hazardous waste sites. Environmental newsletter editor Julie Edelson
argues that EPA's clean-up procedures and standards still need considerable
improvement.

ISSUE 14. Municipal Waste: Is Modern Waste Incineration Technology
an Environmentally Benign Alternative to Garbage
Dumps?   232

YES: Langdon Marsh, from "What Are the Environmental Risks of
Resource Recovery and How Can We Control Them?" *Reclaiming Our
Wastes*, New York Legislative Commission on Solid Waste Manage-
ment   234

NO: Theodore D. Goldfarb, from "Solid Waste Incineration: The Need
for More Stringent Regulation and the Vigorous Pursuit of More
Environmentally Acceptable Means of Solid Waste Disposal," *Reclaiming
Our Wastes*, New York Legislative Commission on Solid Waste
Management   240

Deputy environmental commissioner Langdon Marsh advocates the incineration of municipal garbage as environmentally preferable to landfill disposal. Environmental chemist Goldfarb expresses concern about the
potentially serious health hazards from the toxins emitted during garbage
incineration.

ISSUE 15. Nuclear Waste: Was Yucca Mountain an Appropriate Site for
Nuclear Waste Disposal?   248

YES: Luther J. Carter, from "Siting the Nuclear Waste Repository: Last
Stand at Yucca Mountain," *Environment*   250

NO: Fred C. Shapiro, from "Yucca Mountain," *The New Yorker*   260

Science journalist Luther Carter describes a variety of technical and political
considerations that support the choice of Yucca Mountain for the nuclear

waste dump. Science writer Fred Shapiro contends that the choice of the Yucca site before a thorough technical evaluation was unwise in view of the many political and scientific uncertainties that remain.

ISSUE 16. Do We Need New Federal Legislation to Protect the Future Integrity of Our Groundwater? 274

YES: **David E. Burmaster,** from a review of "Groundwater: Saving the Unseen Resource," *Environment* 276

NO: **Bruce R. Leavitt,** from Statement on behalf of the American Mining Congress before the Subcommittee on Hazardous Wastes and Toxic Substances, U.S. Senate 282

Environmental scientist David Burmaster argues that without new, coordinated federal and state regulatory policies, drinking water supplies will become increasingly contaminated by synthetic organic chemicals. Coal company hydrogeologist Leavitt contends that the variability of hydrogeological conditions and other local considerations make federal groundwater regulation inappropriate.

ISSUE 17. Is Immediate Action Necessary to Minimize Potential Catastrophic Effects of Global Climatic Warming? 288

YES: **Annie Eberhart,** from "If You Can't Stand the Heat," *Public Citizen* 290

NO: **Tom Yulsman,** from "Greenhouse Earth," *Science Digest* 298

Public policy researcher Annie Eberhart urges individual, national, and international action to reduce the possibility of devastating, abrupt effects of greenhouse warming of the Earth. Science news editor Tom Yulsman suggests that the world will have sufficient time to adapt as evidence of the slow onset of climatic change develops.

ISSUE 18. Does the Montreal Ozone Agreement Signal a New Era of International Environmental Statesmanship? 308

YES: **Mostafa K. Tolba,** from "The Ozone Agreement—and Beyond," *Environmental Conservation* 310

NO: **John Gliedman,** from "The Ozone Follies—Is the Pact Too Little, Too Late?" *The Nation* 317

United Nations environmental executive Mostafa Tolba hails the recent agreement reached in Montreal on reducing the consumption of ozone-depleting chemicals as an indication that other worldwide problems, such as

global warming, will be approached in a similar manner. Science writer John Gliedman, while acknowledging the significance of the Montreal pact, does not see signs that the "business as usual" approach to environmental problems is ending.

ISSUE 19. Are Abundant Resources and an Improved Environment Likely Future Prospects for the World's People? 326

YES: Julian L. Simon, from "Life on Earth Is Getting Better, Not Worse," *The Futurist* 328

NO: Lindsey Grant, from "The Cornucopian Fallacies: The Myth of Perpetual Growth," *The Futurist* 334

Economist Julian L. Simon is optimistic about the likelihood that human minds and muscles will overcome resource and environmental problems. Environmental consultant Lindsey Grant fears that unless a "sustainable relationship between people and earth" is developed, the future may bring famine and ecological disaster.

HUMAN SEXUALITY,
Second Edition

ISSUE 1. Is the Sexual Revolution Over?   **2**

YES: John Leo, from "The Sexual Revolution is Over," *Time*   **4**

NO: Barbara Ehrenreich, Elizabeth Hess, and Gloria Jacobs, from
Remaking Love: The Feminization of Sex   **13**

John Leo, a social critic and senior writer for *Time* magazine, brings together statements from a wide variety of family life specialists, sociologists, and sex counselors to defend his claim that the sexual revolution of recent decades, which he describes as an experiment in sexual freedom that failed and has been rejected, is over. Barbara Ehrenreich, Elizabeth Hess, and Gloria Jacobs, all journalists and feminists, claim that a real and irreversible sexual revolution has occurred as to the reinterpretation of sex. This ongoing revolution carries major consequences for our patriarchal, consumerist, and capitalistic society.

**ISSUE 2. Is The "New Woman" the Main Cause of Turmoil and
            Tension in Male/Female Relations Today?**   **20**

YES: Donald Singletary, from "You New Women Want It All!" *Essence* **22**

NO: Betty Winston Baye, from "You Men Want It Both Ways!"
Essence   **28**

Donald Singletary believes women want to be liberated but aren't willing to bear the cost. Since women haven't faced up to what they really want and expect from men, they send out too many confusing signals. Betty Winston Baye believes that the main problem in male/female relationships today is that many men say they want an educated, independent woman with her own career, but when it comes to living in such a relationship, too many of them can't handle this type of woman.

**ISSUE 3. Are Homosexual and Bisexual Relations Natural
            and Normal?**   **34**

YES: Jeannine Gramick, from "Homosexuality and Bisexuality Are as
Natural and Normal as Heterosexuality," an essay written for this
volume   **36**

NO: Robert Gordis, from *Love and Sex*   **45**

Jeannine Gramick, a Catholic nun who works with gay men and lesbians, argues that the main reason many people reject homosexuality and bisexuality as unnatural is that the dominant heterosexual majority believes its lifestyle is the only acceptable orientation. Robert Gordis, biblical professor at the Jewish Theological Seminary in New York, claims that homosexuality is "an abnormality, an illness." He argues for rejecting both the traditional religious reaction to homosexuality as an abomination and the fashionable doctrine that homosexuality is an alternate lifestyle of equal value and legitimacy with heterosexuality.

ISSUE 4. Does Good Sex Require Love?   **56**

YES: Russell Vannoy, from "Some Arguments for Sex With Love,"
Sex Without Love: A Philosophical Exploration   **58**

NO: Russell Vannoy, from "Some Arguments for Sex Without Love,"
Sex Without Love: A Philosophical Exploration   **64**

Russell Vannoy, a philosopher at the State University College of New York at Buffalo, established one of the first courses on the philosophy of sex and love. Here he draws on his skills as a philosopher, on his research, and on class discussions with students to argue both sides of this issue. Vannoy argues that love is the "ultimate aphrodisiac." It gives personal meaning to sex and indicates one is not being treated as a sex object. Love allows us to fulfill a basic need to become totally absorbed with another person. The most powerful need for humans is not sex per se but a relationship, intimacy, acceptance, and affirmation. Vannoy shifts sides, challenging Rollo May's confusion of sex without love with sexual mechanics. Vannoy asks us to examine to what extent the *need* for love is based on personal insecurity, a need for sexual gratification, and a need to conform to societal norms. After exploring feminist suggestions that love is merely a kind of masochistic worship of a woman's oppressor, he points out certain benefits that are available to a nonlover that are often not available to a lover.

ISSUE 5. Is Monogamy the Best Form of Marriage?   **72**

YES: Lisa Davis, from "Vive Monogamy!" *Forum*   **74**

NO: Phyllis Raphael, from "Sexual Exclusivity is Unworkable!" *Forum* **79**

Lisa Davis—pseudonym for a well-known Hollywood screenwriter—has tried a variety of lifestyles and finds monogamy the most satisfying because it provides a sense of continuity, saves energy, promotes personal growth, and ultimately makes true intimacy possible. Novelist and journalist Phyllis

Raphael believes that the American style of exclusive monogamy is an unnatural and unattainable ideal that cripples personal development. She believes that monogamy *with multiple relationships,* in the southern European style, is more realistic for our times.

ISSUE 6. Can Sex Be an Addiction?   84

YES: Patrick Carnes, from "Progress in Sex Addiction: An Addiction Perspective," *SIECUS Report*   86

NO: Martin P. Levine and Richard R. Troiden from "The Myth of Sexual Addiction," an original essay written for this volume   92

Patrick Carnes argues that a significant number of people have identified themselves as sexual addicts—persons with "unstoppable" repetitive behavior patterns that are destructive to the addict and to his or her family. Sexual addiction can best be treated, he claims, by using systems theory and techniques developed by Alcoholics Anonymous, obesity clinics, and substance-abuse rehabilitation programs. Sociologists Martin Levine and Richard Troiden argue that sexual addiction is a myth. The concept, they claim, is culture-bound, highly subjective, and violates the traditional meaning of the medical term *addiction.*

ISSUE 7. Is Sex Education in Schools an Attempt to Institutionalize a Sexual Revolution?   100

YES: Lawrence L. Shornack and Ellen McRoberts Schornack, from "The New Sex Education and the Sexual Revolution: A Critical View," *Family Relations*   102

NO: Peter Scales, from "Sense and Nonsense About Sexuality Education: A Rejoinder," *Family Relations*   109

Lawrence Shornack, a sociologist, and Ellen Shornack, a child and family therapist, argue that the new sex education attempts to institutionalize the sexual revolution by indoctrinating students in the ideology of sexual permissiveness. Peter Scales, director of education for the Planned Parenthood Federation of America, rejects the Shornacks' argument, pointing out that it contains serious misrepresentations, myths, inaccuracies, distortions, and innuendos used to buttress a shaky thesis.

ISSUE 8. Are School-Based Health Clinics an Effective Way of Reducing Teenage Pregnancies and STDs?   120

YES: Richard Kenney, from "School-Based Health Clinics Meet the Needs of Today's Adolescents," an essay written for this volume   122

NO: Phyllis Schlafly, from "School-Based Sex Clinics vs. Sex Respect," *The Phyllis Schlafly Report*   129

Richard Kenney, director of ambulatory pediatrics and adolescent medicine at Charlotte Memorial Hospital in North Carolina, argues from his experiences at such clinics that they appear able to address some of the problems faced by adolescents in a cost-effective and medically efficacious manner. In preventing pregnancy, they save $25 for every dollar spent. Phyllis Schlafly, founder of the Eagle Forum, claims that sex education and the associated health clinics have been promoted by some educators and social workers to provide themselves with jobs. Rather than encouraging teenage abstinence, this education has legitimized teenage promiscuity and caused the rise in teenage pregnancies since the 1950s.

ISSUE 9. Should Prenatal Testing for Sex Selection Be Permitted?   138

YES: Peter Singer and Deane Wells, from *Making Babies: The New Science and Ethics of Conception*   140

NO: Gena Corea, from *The Mother Machine: Reproductive Technologies from Artificial Insemination to Artificial Wombs*   144

Peter Singer, director of the Centre for Human Bioethics at Monash University in Australia, and Deane Wells, a member of the Australian Parliament, emphasize that the benefits sex selection techniques would have in promoting population control outweigh alarmist claims about an unbalanced sex ratio. Gena Corea, founder of the Feminist International Network on the New Reproductive Technologies, argues that the immediate and most socially devastating outcome of the new techniques for predetermining or selecting the sex of fetuses is "gynicide," her term for the deliberate and systematic extermination of women.

ISSUE 10. Will AIDS Become a Middle-Class Heterosexual Disease? 154

YES: Ann Giudici Fettner, from "The Facts About Straight Sex and AIDS," *The Village Voice*   156

NO: Randy Shilts, from "The Facts About Straight Sex and AIDS," *The Village Voice*   159

Ann Giudici Fettner, a prominent journalist and contributor to *The Village Voice*, a New York City newspaper, points out that AIDS became a heterosexual disease as early as 1979 when the first heterosexual woman was infected with the HIV virus by her male partner. Since our statistics are not reliable and real risk estimates are impossible, AIDS must be regarded as a crapshoot for heterosexuals with a potentially deadly payoff. Given the numbers, and

until all the facts are in, heterosexuals who are not strictly and mutually monogamous should protect themselves with condoms and spermicidal nonoxynol-9. Randy Shilts, author of *And the Band Played On: Politics, People and the AIDS Epidemic*, argues that the news media has tried to mainstream AIDS by convincing heterosexuals that the disease is going to sweep through the heterosexual community the way it did through the gay community in the early 1980s. Despite the fact that there are high numbers of infected heterosexuals in certain parts of the country, Shilts maintains that "This is never going to be a middle-class heterosexual disease." Geographic location and social factors like being a black or Hispanic woman, being involved in IV-drug use, and living in inner-city ghettos greatly increase a heterosexual's risk of developing the disease.

ISSUE 11. Is The Antiabortion Movement Based on a Belief in the Sacredness of Human Life?   164
YES: Orrin G. Hatch, from *The Value of Life*   166
NO: James W. Prescott, from "The Abortion of 'The Silent Scream,' " *The Humanist*   176

Senator Orrin G. Hatch argues that abortion is a worldwide calamity. He supports a constitutional amendment that will overturn the U.S. Supreme Court decisions legalizing abortion and halt what he sees as the carnage of abortion by restoring respect for all human life as a right protected under our Constitution. Despite the claims of the antichoice advocates that they are pro-life, James W. Prescott, a developmental neuropsychologist and cross-cultural psychologist, argues that their real motivation comes from an authoritarianism that consistently supports human violence, is indifferent to pain and suffering, and denies the personal right of self-determination, especially in sexual issues.

ISSUE 12. Is Rape Motivated by Agression Instead of Sex?   186
YES: A. Nicholas Groth, from *Men Who Rape*   188
NO: Craig T. Palmer, from "Twelve Reasons Why Rape Is Not Sexually Motivated: A Skeptical Examination," *Journal of Sex Research*   193

A. Nicholas Groth argues that rape is always and foremost an aggressive act. While sexual pleasure may sometime be a factor, rape is primarily motivated by the rapist's anger, frustration, and rage; his compulsive need for control; and, in some cases, by sadism. Craig T. Palmer claims that the arguments that present rape as being motivated primarily by anger, rage, the need for power, or sadism are flawed. He examines twelve arguments and finds them

illogical, based on inaccurate definitions, untestable, or inconsistent with the actual behavior of rapists.

ISSUE 13. Does Pornography Promote Sexual Violence? 202

YES: **Hilary Johnson,** from "Pornography Panel Discussion," *Vogue* 204

NO: **Carole S. Vance,** from "Pornography Panel Discussion," *Vogue* 209

Hilary Johnson, a free-lance writer, claims that lawyers and feminist organizations are beginning to compile evidence that they believe irrefutably links pornography and male sexual violence. Carole S. Vance, an anthropologist, argues that large-scale studies have failed to demonstrate a clear relationship between pornography and violence against women.

ISSUE 14. Does Government Have a Constitutional Right to Prohibit Certain Kinds of Sexual Conduct? 218

YES: **Byron White,** from the Majority Opinion, *Bowers v. Hardwick,* U.S. Supreme Court 220

NO: **Harry Blackmun,** from the Dissenting Opinion, *Bowers v. Hardwick,* U.S. Supreme Court 224

Justice White, arguing the majority opinion, claims that, unlike heterosexuals, homosexuals do not have a constitutional right to privacy when it comes to engaging in oral or anal sex, even in the privacy of their homes, because of the traditional social and legal condemnation of sodomy. Justice Blackmun, dissenting from the majority opinion, argues that since the right to be left alone is the most comprehensive of human rights and the most valued by civilized people, the state has no right or reason to prohibit any sexual acts engaged in privately by consenting adults.

ISSUE 15. Should State-Supported Family Life Education Programs Stress Premarital Chastity and Monogamy? 230

YES: **Marion Crecco,** from press releases supporting New Jersey Assembly Bill 3306 232

NO: **Susan Wilson,** from a statement to the New Jersey State Legislature denouncing Assembly Bill 3306 234

Marion Crecco, Republican assemblywoman in New Jersey, has sponsored a bill requiring all public school teachers to stress premarital sexual abstinence and sexually exclusive monogamy in all courses and programs dealing with AIDS. Susan N. Wilson, a former member of the New Jersey State Board of

Education, argues that laws requiring teachers to stress sexual abstinence before marriage and sexual exclusivity in marriage look deceptively appealing. She believes, however, that in the long term, this approach is flawed and will actually increase the number of AIDS victims and the number of unintended pregnancies among teenagers.

ISSUE 16. Should Our Society Recognize Nonmarital and Gay Unions?   **240**

YES: Nelson S. T. Thayer, from the Task Force Report on Changing Patterns of Sexuality and Family Life, *The Voice*   **242**

NO: Ruth Tiffany Barnhouse, from "Lasting Heterosexual Marriage Is Still the Paradigm Despite Failures," *The Episcopalian*   **250**

Nelson S. T. Thayer and the twelve members of his task force outline ten major social and cultural changes in American society that have occurred over the past fifty years, biblical and theological considerations, the history of marriage, and new understandings of the person—all as a preface to recommending that the church, and, by implication, our civil laws, should recognize the nonmarital sexual relationships of young singles and "post-married" adults, alternatives to traditional exclusive monogamy, and homosexual couples. Ruth Tiffany Barnhouse, a professor at Perkins School of Theology, Dallas, Texas, and an Episcopal priest, argues that the basic principles of western civilization, rooted in the Judaeo–Christian tradition, cannot change. Long-term heterosexual monogamy, she argues, is the only acceptable paradigm. Recognition of homosexual unions and nonmarital or nonexclusive heterosexual marriages would violate those essential principles.

ISSUE 17. Should Prostitution Be Decriminalized?   **256**

YES: Julie Pearl, from "The Highest Paying Customers: America's Cities and the Costs of Prostitution Control," *Hastings Law Review*   **258**

NO: Charles Winick, from "Debate on Legalization of Prostitution," *Medical Aspects of Human Sexuality*   **266**

Law student Julie Pearl argues that we are paying too high a financial and social cost for the ineffective enforcement of laws against prostitution. The money and law enforcement personnel freed by decriminalizing prostitution could be better used to protect citizens against violent crimes. Charles Winick, coauthor of *The Lively Commerce—Prostitution in the United States*, argues that it would be "extremely foolhardy to base public policy on the temporary or neurotic needs of a very small element of the population." Whether prostitution is legal or illegal, it is always surrounded by an array of socially undesirable third parties, by pimps, violence, blackmail, and drugs.

ISSUE 18. Do Surrogate Motherhood Contracts Exploit Women? 272

YES: Susan Ince, from *Test-Tube Women* 274

NO: Lori B. Andrews, from "Removing the Stigma of Surrogate Motherhood," *Family Advocate* 285

Women's health counselor Susan Ince recounts her personal experience of being interviewed for surrogate motherhood. She believes surrogate motherhood for pay should be banned because it exploits women and is a form of reproductive prostitution. Lori B. Andrews, a research attorney at the American Bar Foundation, argues that despite the many legal conflicts and complications of surrogate motherhood, society must consider the right to privacy and self-determination of a childless couple.

LEGAL ISSUES,
Third Edition

ISSUE 1. Should the Adversary System Be Abolished?   **2**

YES: Anne Strick, from *Injustice for All*   **4**

NO: Monroe Freedman, from *Lawyers' Ethics in an Adversary System*   **12**

Writer Anne Strick cites cases to support her view that the adversary system produces results that hide the truth and fail to do justice. Professor of law Monroe Freedman defends the system by arguing that justice emerges from the clash of strongly defended positions.

ISSUE 2. Is There a Litigation Crisis?   **20**

YES: Bayless Manning, from "Hyperlexis: Our National Disease," *Northwestern Law Review*   **22**

NO: Marc Galanter, from "The Day After the Litigation Explosion," *Maryland Law Review*   **33**

Former Stanford Law School dean Bayless Manning contends that our society and our legal system are suffering from too great a reliance on law to settle disputes. Law professor Marc Galanter contends that court statistics do not support complaints about excessive litigation and that litigation provides some benefits to society.

ISSUE 3. Should Plea Bargaining Be Abolished?   **48**

YES: Kenneth Kipnis, from "Criminal Justice and the Negotiated Plea," *Ethics*   **50**

NO: John R. Wheatley, from "Plea Bargaining—A Case for Its Continuance," *Massachusetts Law Quarterly*   **63**

Professor of philosophy Kenneth Kipnis makes the case that justice cannot be traded on the open market and that plea bargaining often subverts the cause of justice. John Wheatley, former district attorney, contends that plea bargaining can result in a savings of time, money, and effort and that guilty persons go to jail as a result.

ISSUE 4. Should the Police Do More to Manage Street Life?   **72**

YES: James Q. Wilson and George L. Kelling, from "Broken Windows," *The Atlantic Monthly*   **74**

NO: Carl B. Klockars, from "Order Maintenance, the Quality of Urban Life, and Police: A Different Line of Argument," William Geller, ed., *Police Leadership in America*   85

Political scientists James Q. Wilson and George L. Kelling claim that the police can provide more protection to citizens by increasing foot patrols and other programs that involve them more in the life of the community. Criminologist Carl B. Klockars argues that such "order maintenance" programs would involve a substantial threat to individual freedom and the rule of law.

ISSUE 5. Is the Legal Profession Declining?   96

YES: L. Harold Levinson, from "Making Society's Legal System Accessbile to Society: The Lawyer's Role and Its Implications," *Vanderbilt Law Review*   98

NO: James W. Jones, from "The Challenge of Change: The Practice of Law in the Year 2000," *Vanderbilt Law Review*   103

Law professor L. Harold Levinson discusses changes in the legal profession and warns against many of the current trends developing, which he believes run counter to what it means to be a lawyer. James W. Jones, a partner in a Washington, D.C., law firm, outlines the changes in the practice of law and applauds the services that law firms are beginning to offer and the changing role of the lawyer.

ISSUE 6. Does Drug Use Testing Violate the Fourth Amendment?   114

YES: Lois G. Williams, from "Statement by the Director of Litigation for the National Treasury Employees Union," U.S. Congress, House, Subcommittee on Human Resources of the Committee on Post Office and Civil Service   116

NO: Judge Alvin B. Rubin, from *National Treasury Employees Union v. Von Raab*, U.S. Court of Appeals for the Fifth Circuit   123

Attorney Lois Williams claims that mandatory drug testing of federal employees is unwarranted and unreasonable and, therefore, a violation of the Fourth Amendment. Federal judge Alvin Rubin argues that, while mandatory drug testing is a search covered by the Fourth Amendment, drug testing is not an unreasonable or unconstitutional search.

ISSUE 7. Is It Unconstitutional to Discriminate Against Homosexuals?   132

YES: Judge William Norris, from Majority Opinion, *Watkins v. U.S. Army*, U.S. Court of Appeals for the Ninth Circuit   134

NO: Judge Stephen Reinhardt, from Minority Opinion, *Watkins v. U.S. Army*, U.S. Court of Appeals for the Ninth Circuit   **148**

Federal Court of Appeals judge William Norris holds that homosexuals are a class protected from discrimination by the Equal Protection clause of the Constitution. Judge Stephen Reinhardt, in dissent, argues that recent Supreme Court rulings suggest that homosexuals are not a constitutionally protected class.

ISSUE 8. Should Prayer Be Permitted in Public Schools?   **156**

YES: Charles E. Rice, from "The Prayer Amendment: A Justification," *South Carolina Law Review*   **158**

NO: William J. Brennan, Jr., from Concurring Opinion, *School District of Abington Township, Pennsylvania v. Schempp*   **167**

Professor Charles Rice argues that it is permissible and important for prayer to be allowed in schools. Supreme Court justice William Brennan details his view that religion and government must not mix or both will suffer.

ISSUE 9. Should There Be a Right to Abortion?   **178**

YES: Harry Blackmun, from Majority Opinion, *Roe v. Wade*, U.S. Supreme Court   **180**

NO: John Noonan, Jr., from "Why a Constitutional Amendment?" *Human Life Review*   **193**

Supreme Court justice Harry Blackmun refers to historical attitudes, medical opinion, and legal precedent to defend the right of abortion. Professor of law John Noonan expresses his fear that the courts have taken upon themselves the power to define a human being, and that this will have dangerous and undesirable consequences.

ISSUE 10. Should Pornography Be Protected by the First Amendment?   **204**

YES: Frank Easterbrook, from *American Booksellers Association, Inc., v. Hudnut*, U.S. Court of Appeals for the Seventh District   **206**

NO: Andrea Dworkin, from *Amicus Curiae, American Booksellers Association, Inc., v. Hudnut*, U.S. Court of Appeals for the Seventh District   **214**

Judge Frank Easterbrook holds that an ordinance regulating pornography is an unconstitutional infringement on freedom of speech and press. Author Andrea Dworkin maintains that pornography should not be constitutionally

protected because it is destructive, abusive, and detrimental to women, and violates their civil rights.

ISSUE 11. Is Affirmative Action Constitutional? 224

YES: Justice Thurgood Marshall, from Dissenting Opinion, *Regents of the University of California v. Allan Bakke*, U.S. Supreme Court 226

NO: Justice Potter Stewart, From Dissenting Opinion, *Fullilove v. Klutznick*, U.S. Supreme Court 235

Supreme Court justice Thurgood Marshall points to past discrimination and argues that we must find a way to compensate for the years of disadvantage. Justice Potter Stewart contends that the law and the Constitution must not discriminate on the basis of race, for whatever reason.

ISSUE 12. Should Surrogate Motherhood Contracts Be Illegal? 240

YES: Chief Justice Robert Wilentz, from *In the Matter of Baby M*, New Jersey Supreme Court 242

NO: Noel Keane and Dennis Breo, from *The Surrogate Mother* 254

Judge Robert Wilentz holds that it is illegal for a "surrogate mother" to agree to sell her maternal rights. Lawyer Noel Keane and writer Dennis Breo argue that surrogate motherhood contracts are not baby selling and should be allowed by states.

ISSUE 13. Do Patients Have a Right to Die? 266

YES: Judge Paul Liacos, from Majority Opinion, *Brophy v. New England Sinai Hospital, Inc.*, Massachusetts Supreme Judicial Court 268

NO: Judge Neil Lynch, from Dissenting Opinion, *Brophy v. New England Sinai Hospital, Inc.*, Massachusetts Supreme Judicial Court 278

Judge Paul Liacos rules that the family of a person in a "persistent vegetative state" may stop providing care even if that leads to the death of the patient. Judge Neil Lynch believes that there is no constitutional right to die that permits the family to deny food and water to the patient.

ISSUE 14. Should the Death Penalty Be Abolished? 286

YES: Jack Greenberg, from "Against the American System of Capital Punishment," *Harvard Law Review* 288

NO: Earnest van den Haag, from "The Ultimate Punishment: A Defense," *Harvard Law Review* 295

Law professor Jack Greenberg argues that capital punishment should be banned because it is applied erratically and in a racially and regionally biased manner. Professor van den Haag responds that the death penalty is moral and just and should be employed against those who commit murder.

ISSUE 15. Should the Exclusionary Rule Be Abolished?   302

YES: Malcolm Richard Wilkey, from "The Exclusionary Rule: Why Suppress Valid Evidence?" *Judicature*   304

NO: Yale Kamisar, from "The Exclusionary Rule in Historical Perspective: The Struggle to Make the Fourth Amendment More Than 'an Empty Blessing,' " *Judicature*   316

U.S. Court of Appeals judge Malcolm Wilkey raises objections to the exclusionary rule on the grounds that it may suppress evidence and allow the guilty to go free. Professor Yale Kamisar argues that the exclusionary rule is necessary to prevent abuses by police and to protect citizens' rights.

ISSUE 16. Should Handguns Be Banned?   328

YES: Josh Sugarmann, from "The NRA Is Right, But We Still Need to Ban Handguns," *Washington Monthly*   330

NO: James D. Wright, from "Second Thoughts About Gun Control," *Public Interest*   336

Writer Josh Sugarmann claims that handguns should be banned for public health reasons, even if such a ban might not stop criminals from obtaining weapons. Professor of sociology James Wright concludes, after examining how guns are used, that banning guns would not be beneficial.

ISSUE 17. Should the Insanity Defense Be Abolished?   348

YES: Jonathan Rowe, from "Why Liberals Should Hate the Insanity Defense," *Washington Monthly*   350

NO: Richard Bonnie, from *Statement Submitted to the Committee on the Judiciary,* United States Senate   360

Editor Jonathan Rowe examines the insanity defense as it is now administered and finds that it is most likely to be used by white middle- or upper-class defendants and that its application is unfair and leads to unjust results. Professor of law Richard Bonnie argues that the abolition of the insanity defense would be immoral and leave no alternative for those who are not responsible for their actions.

MORAL ISSUES,
First Edition

ISSUE 1. Is Morality Relative? 2

YES: William Graham Sumner, from *Folkways: A Study of the Sociological Importance of Usages, Manners, Customs, Mores and Morals* 4

NO: James Rachels, from *Elements of Moral Philosophy* 12

Pioneering American sociologist William Graham Sumner argues that morality is not absolute but is a social and cultural phenomenon that varies according to the customs and mores of different cultural groups. But philosopher James Rachels vehemently disagrees and shows in his article that certain particular values must be maintained by *any* society.

ISSUE 2. Is Morality Subjective? 20

YES: Bertrand Russell, from *Religion and Science* 22

NO: Brand Blanshard, from "The New Subjectivism in Ethics," *Philosophy and Phenomenological Research* 28

British philosopher Bertrand Russell holds that morality is subjective, that moral judgments express personal emotions, and that differences in value judgments are due to differences in taste. American philosopher Brand Blanshard rejects all of these views and maintains that subjectivism in ethics is untenable.

ISSUE 3. Is Morality the Exclusive Province of Religion? 36

YES: Emil Brunner, from *The Divine Imperative: A Study in Christian Ethics* 38

NO: John Arthur, from "Morality Without God," *Contemporary Readings in Social and Political Ethics* 45

Swiss theologian Emil Brunner writes that there is no understanding of "the good" except in terms of obedience to the will of God. American philosopher John Arthur claims, however, that morality is independent of religion.

ISSUE 4. Should One Always Follow One's Conscience?   **54**

YES: Hastings Rashdall, from "Moral Philosophy and Moral
Authority," *Conscience and Christ: Six Lectures on Christian Ethics*   **56**

NO: Jonathan Bennett, from "The Conscience of Huckleberry Finn,"
Philosophy   **64**

Hastings Rashdall supports the view that conscience is a rational faculty
within each person, which determines judgments of right and wrong.
Jonathan Bennett distinguishes between conscience and feelings of sympa-
thy, and holds that in some cases these feelings must take priority over
conscience.

ISSUE 5. Do the Ends Justify the Means?   **72**

YES: J. J. C. Smart, from "An Outline of a System of Utilitarian
Ethics," *Utilitarianism: For and Against*   **74**

NO: Paul W. Taylor, from "A Problem for Utilitarianism," *Principles of
Ethics: An Introduction*   **80**

Australian philosopher J. J. C. Smart defends the principle that one ought to
act in such a way as to promote, as a result, the greatest happiness for the
greatest number. This end result can be used to justify all actions. American
philosopher Paul Taylor objects to this utilitarian position on the grounds
that it does not take proper notice of the principles of justice.

ISSUE 6. Do We Have a Moral Right to Die?   **88**

YES: Eliot Slater, from "Choosing the Time to Die," *Proceedings of the
Fifth Annual Conference for Suicide Prevention*   **90**

NO: Herbert Hendin, from *Suicide in America*   **94**

Eliot Slater, a British psychiatrist, argues that individuals do have a right to
die and that those who wish to exercise this right should be allowed to do so.
American psychiatrist Herbert Hendin contends that suicide is an unhealthy
response to the problems of life and that this impulse is often temporary and
should not be supported.

ISSUE 7. Is Euthanasia Immoral?   **102**

YES: J. Gay-Williams, from "The Wrongfulness of Euthanasia,"
Intervention and Reflection: Basic Issues in Medical Ethics   **104**

NO: Baruch A. Brody, from "A Non-Consequentialist Argument for
Active Euthanasia," *Beneficent Euthanasia*   **108**

J. Gay-Williams believes that euthanasia is immoral because it is a violation of one's natural will to survive. Additionally, he points out that a public policy allowing euthanasia will have severely negative consequences. But Baruch A. Brody, a medical ethicist, argues that euthanasia is morally permissible, as shown by an examination of the concepts of consent, agency, and the right to life.

ISSUE 8. Is Abortion Always Immoral? 116

YES: John T. Noonan, Jr., from "An Almost Absolute Value in History," *The Morality of Abortion: Legal and Historical Perspectives* 118

NO: Jane English, from "Abortion and the Concept of a Person," *Canadian Journal of Philosophy* 124

In the debate on this volatile issue, John T. Noonan, Jr., a professor of law, holds that once a being is conceived by human parents and has a human genetic code, it is a full human being and cannot morally be destroyed. Philosopher Jane English argues that there is no well-defined line dividing persons from non-persons. She claims that both the conservative and the liberal positions are too extreme, and that some abortions are morally justifiable and some are not.

ISSUE 9. Is Extramarital Sex Wrong? 134

YES: Norman L. Geisler, from *Ethics: Alternatives and Issues* 136

NO: Richard Taylor, from *Having Love Affairs* 143

Normal L. Geisler, a Christian ethicist, describes sex as a powerful force, which can only lead to corruption unless confined within the bounds of marriage. Philosopher Richard Taylor holds that love affairs can be a source of great joy, even if they can also be dangerous for married people. He supports the right of each individual to decide whether or not to engage in them.

ISSUE 10. Do We Have a Moral Responsibility to Rehabilitate Criminals? 154

YES: Karl Menninger, from "The Crime of Punishment," *Saturday Review* 156

NO: C. S. Lewis, from "The Humanitarian Theory of Punishment," *God in the Dock* 163

Psychiatrist Karl Menninger argues that a therapeutic attitude should replace the vindictive approach we have toward criminals and that treatment should

replace punishment. Religious writer C. S. Lewis disagrees with this so-called humanitarian approach. Justice requires that criminals deserve, and should receive, punishment.

ISSUE 11. Should Capital Punishment Be Abolished?   **170**

YES: Arthur Koestler, from *Reflections on Hanging*   **172**

NO: Ernest van den Haag, from "On Deterrence and the Death Penalty," *Journal of Criminal Law and Criminology*   **180**

Novelist and social critic Arthur Koestler argues for the abolition of capital punishment because it has no special deterrent effect and serves no useful purpose. Psychoanalyst and philosopher Ernest van den Haag argues for the retention of the death penalty because the statistics on deterrence are not clear. He thinks we act rashly if we abolish capital punishment and consequently bring about an increase in crime.

ISSUE 12. Is Pornography a Threat to Society?   **188**

YES: Charles H. Keating, Jr., from "Report of Commissioner Keating," *The Report of the Commission on Obscenity and Pornography*   **190**

NO: G. L. Simons, from *Pornography Without Prejudice*   **197**

Charles H. Keating, Jr., was a member of the 1970 congressional Commission on Obscenity and Pornography. He maintains that pornography corrupts and that the moral decay brought on by pornography is a threat to society. But G. L. Simons, an English writer on sex-related topics, claims that there is no evidence to show any harm that could outweigh pornography's benefits—namely, that some people enjoy pornography and learn from it.

ISSUE 13. Should the Law Enforce Morality?   **204**

YES: Sir Patrick Devlin, from "The Enforcement of Morals," *Proceedings of the British Academy*   **206**

NO: H. L. A. Hart, from "Immorality and Treason," *The Listener*   **214**

Sir Patrick Devlin, a leading British judge, argues that society requires morality and that the law is fully justified in supporting common morality against offenders. H. L. A. Hart, a former professor of jurisprudence at Oxford University, defends the idea of a realm of privacy, proper to each individual, into which the law cannot rightfully enter.

ISSUE 14. Is Affirmative Action Morally Justifiable?　　220

YES: **Thomas Nagel,** from "A Defense of Affirmative Action,"
Testimony Before the Senate Subcommittee on the Constitution　　222

NO: **Lisa H. Newton,** from "Reverse Discrimination as Unjustified,"
Ethics　　227

In testimony before a Senate subcommittee on the Constitution, philosopher Thomas Nagel argues for "strong" affirmative action for blacks. Philosopher Lisa H. Newton holds that all such programs are cases of reverse discrimination, and thus cases of discrimination, and thus unjust.

ISSUE 15. Are Profits the Only Business of Business?　　234

YES: **Milton Friedman,** from "The Social Responsibility of Business Is to Increase Its Profits," *The New York Times Magazine*　　236

NO: **Christopher D. Stone,** from *Where the Law Ends: The Social Control of Corporate Behavior*　　242

Economist Milton Friedman argues that business has no social responsibility beyond profit-seeking. But Christopher Stone, a professor of law, objects that the marketplace and the law are insufficient to induce socially responsible behavior in corporations.

ISSUE 16. Does Society Have an Obligation to Care for the Less Well Off?　　250

YES: **Trudy Govier,** from "The Right to Eat and the Duty to Work,"
Philosophy of the Social Sciences　　252

NO: **Irving Kristol,** from "Social Justice" and "The Poverty of Redistribution," *Two Cheers for Capitalism*　　261

Trudy Govier, a Canadian philosopher, argues that society does have an obligation to directly care for the less well off. Irving Kristol, author and social critic, argues that society should not redistribute wealth to the less well off but should promote economic growth in general.

ISSUE 17. Do Rich Nations Have an Obligation to Help Poor Nations?　　270

YES: **Peter Singer,** from *Practical Ethics*　　272

NO: **Garrett Hardin,** from "Lifeboat Ethics: The Case Against Helping the Poor," *Psychology Today*　　280

Australian philosopher Peter Singer takes the position that rich nations can help poor nations without harm to themselves and that therefore they *should* help. Biologist Garrett Hardin argues that since the birthrates of poor nations are high and the earth's resources finite, future generations of all nations will be hurt if wealthy nations assist poor ones and thereby support and maintain high birthrates.

ISSUE 18. Does Morality Require Nuclear Disarmament?   290

YES: Douglas P. Lackey, from "Missiles and Morals: A Utilitarian Look at Nuclear Deterrence," *Philosophy and Public Affairs*   292

NO: Gregory S. Kavka, from "Doubts about Unilateral Nuclear Disarmament," *Philosophy and Public Affairs*   300

Douglas P. Lackey, professor of philosophy at Baruch College, argues that nuclear disarmament is the best strategy open to the United States from both moral and military points of view. Gregory S. Kavka, professor of philosophy at the University of California at Irvine, doubts that Lackey and other proponents of unilateral nuclear disarmament have taken sufficient account of the likelihood of Soviet expansionism if this policy were adopted.

POLITICAL ISSUES,
Sixth Edition

ISSUE 1. Is America Ruled by an Elite?   2

YES: G. William Domhoff, from *Who Rules America Now?*   4

NO: Andrew M. Greeley, from *Building Coalitions*   13

Sociologist G. William Domhoff sees American political life in terms of elite domination. Sociologist Andrew M. Greeley believes that there is no single, established center of power and points to the behavior of the system as evidence.

ISSUE 2. Have American Political Parties Lost Their Power?   20

YES: Nelson W. Polsby, from *Consequences of Party Reform*   22

NO: Xandra Kayden and Eddie Mahe, Jr., from *The Party Goes On: The Persistence of the Two-Party System in the United States*   29

Nelson Polsby, a political scientist, believes that the presidential nominating process and the influence of television have contributed to a sharp decline in the influence of political parties. Xandra Kayden and Eddie Mahe, Jr., maintain that parties have not declined, but changed, becoming more national, more professional, and more important in running campaigns.

ISSUE 3. Do Political Action Committees Undermine Democracy?   38

YES: Fred Wertheimer, from "Campaign Finance Reform: The Unfinished Agenda," *Annals of the American Academy*   40

NO: Phyllis Schlafly, from "PACs Protect Political Participation," *The Phyllis Schlafly Report*   44

Fred Wertheimer, president of Common Cause, argues that PACs exert too much influence over the electoral process, allowing special interests to get the ear of elected officials at the expense of the national interest. Conservative activist Phyllis Schlafly defends PACs because they are a means of exercising the right to free speech and because they permit conservative voices to be heard during political campaigns.

ISSUE 4. Do the News Media Have a Liberal Bias?   52

YES: William Rusher, from *The Coming Battle for the Media*   54

NO: Edward S. Herman and Noam Chomsky, from "Propaganda Mill," *The Progressive* **60**

William Rusher, a media analyst and publisher of the *National Review*, argues that the media are biased against conservatives and that news coverage promotes liberal opinions. Professors Edward Herman and Noam Chomsky critique the mass media from the perspective of the left and find the media to be a "propaganda mill" in the service of the wealthy and powerful.

ISSUE 5. Should Congress Be Reformed? **70**

YES: Gregg Easterbrook, from "What's Wrong with Congress?" *Atlantic Monthly* **72**

NO: Gary Orfield, from *Congressional Power: Congress and Social Change* **83**

Journalist Gregg Easterbrook believes that before Congress can lead the nation, it must be able to lead itself, and it has notably failed to do so. Gary Orfield, of Brookings Institute, argues that Congress does a good job of reflecting the attitudes and trends of the electorate as a whole.

ISSUE 6. Should We Examine the Private Lives of Presidential Candidates? **92**

YES: Gail Sheehy, from *Character: America's Search for Leadership* **94**

NO: Richard Sennett, from "A Republic of Souls," *Harper's Magazine* **98**

Journalist Gail Sheehy argues that character has always played a role in selecting our presidents and that it has been a critical factor in determining how well our presidents have performed in office. Richard Sennett, a writer and sociologist, rejects personal scrutiny as a puritanical compulsion that keeps Americans from concentrating on the substance of the issues that will confront the president and the nation.

ISSUE 7. Has Congress Restricted Presidential War Powers Too Much? **104**

YES: Barry Goldwater, from "A Sound Legislative Power?" *Congressional Digest* **106**

NO: Jacob K. Javits, from "War Powers Reconsidered," *Foreign Affairs* **110**

Former Arizona senator Goldwater argues that, while Congress can "declare" war, only the president can "make" war. Only the president can act with adequate force and speed to protect national security. Jacob Javits, the late senator from New York, maintains that the War Powers Act reaffirms the intention of the Constitution to ensure that the effective power to make war originates in the will of Congress.

ISSUE 8. Does the Government Regulate Too Much?   118

YES: Barry Crickmer, from "Regulation: How Much Is Enough?"
Nation's Business   120

NO: Susan and Martin Tolchin, from *Dismantling America*   126

Editor Barry Crickmer argues that the interests of citizens and consumers could be better served by the forces of the profit motive than by government intervention. Martin and Susan Tolchin contend that without vigorous regulation businesses will destroy the environment and endanger lives in their single-minded pursuit of profit.

ISSUE 9. Does the Supreme Court Abuse Its Power?   136

YES: Joseph Sobran, from "Minority Rule," *The National Review*   138
NO: William J. Brennan, Jr., from "The Constitution of the United
States: Contemporary Ratification," *Symposium conducted at Georgetown
University*   143

Journalist Joseph Sobran believes that the Supreme Court has inverted its original role and now wields the arbitrary power it was intended to check. Willilam J. Brennan, Jr., a Supreme Court justice, holds that judges have a duty to interpret the Constitution and to protect the democratic process.

ISSUE 10. Will Tougher Sentencing Reduce Crime?   154

YES: James Q. Wilson, from *Thinking About Crime*   156

NO: Linda Rocawich, from "Lock 'Em Up: America's All-Purpose
Cure for Crime," *The Progressive*   169

Political scientist James Q. Wilson says that the prospect of swift and certain punishment is more likely to reduce violent crime than are social programs aimed at relieving poverty. Journalist Linda Rocawich contends that locking people up is inhumane, is often applied in a racially discriminatory manner, and does not deter crime.

ISSUE 11. Is Capital Punishment Justified?   178

YES: Walter Berns, from *For Capital Punishment: Crime and the
Morality of the Death Penalty*   180

NO: Donal E. J. MacNamara, from "The Case Against Capital
Punishment," *Social Action*   187

Professor Walter Berns is convinced that the death penalty has a place in modern society and that it serves a need now, as it did when the Constitu-

tion was framed. Criminologist Donal MacNamara presents a ten-point argument against capital punishment, raising ethical and practical questions concerning the death penalty.

ISSUE 12. Is Affirmative Action Reverse Discrimination?   **196**

YES: Glenn C. Loury, from "Beyond Civil Rights," *The New Republic*   **198**

NO: Herman Schwartz, from "In Defense of Affirmative Action,"
Dissent   **205**

Harvard professor Glenn Loury contends that insistence on "ill-suited" civil rights strategies makes it impossible for blacks to achieve full equality in American society. Law professor Herman Schwartz argues that we must somehow undo the cruel consequences of racism that still plague our society and its victims.

ISSUE 13. Should Workers Be Paid According to "Comparable Worth"?   **212**

YES: Ronnie Steinberg and Lois Haignere, from "Now Is the Time for Pay Equity," *Gender at Work*   **214**

NO: Geoffrey Cowley, from "Comparable Worth: Another Terrible Idea," *Washington Monthly*   **219**

Feminist writers Ronnie Steinberg and Lois Haignere advocate redesigning pay scales in order to "correct the practice of paying women and minorities less than white men for work that requires equivalent skills, responsibilities, stresses, personal contacts, and working conditions." Geoffrey Cowley, a newspaper columnist, claims that it is impossible to calculate "comparable worth" and that the effort to do so will create a confusing, bureaucratic tangle and lead to greater inequities.

ISSUE 14. Does Our Welfare System Hurt the Poor?   **228**

YES: Charles Murray, from *Losing Ground: American Social Policy, 1950–1980*   **230**

NO: William Julius Wilson, from *The Truly Disadvantaged: The Inner City, the Underclass, and Public Policy*   **237**

Political scientist Charles Murray maintains that the best welfare policy, at least for able-bodied working-age people, is no welfare support by the government. Professor William Julius Wilson argues that welfare policy has *not* contributed to economic decline for the poor; what has had an effect on poverty rates are social changes leading to a sharp rise in black male unemployment.

ISSUE 15. Does Government Have a Right to Prohibit Homosexual
Acts? 246

YES: Justice Byron R. White, from Majority Opinion, *Bowers v.
Hardwick*, U.S. Supreme Court 248

NO: Justice Harry Blackmun, et al., from Dissenting Opinion,
Bowers v. Hardwick, U.S. Supreme Court 252

The majority opinion of the Supreme Court contends that states may outlaw homosexual conduct without violating the Constitution because in our Western tradition there is no fundamental right to engage in homosexual acts. Justice Harry Blackmun and three other members of the Supreme Court contend that the State violates the Constitution whenever it attempts to regulate or ban sexual acts that take place in the privacy of the home.

ISSUE 16. Abortion: Should Public Officials Protect the "Right to
Choose"? 258

YES: Mario Cuomo, from "Religious Belief and Public Morality: A
Catholic Governor's Perspective," *Address to the Department of Theology,
University of Notre Dame* 260

NO: Henry Hyde, from "Keeping God in the Closet: Some Thoughts
on the Exorcism of Religious Values From Public Life," *Address to the
University of Notre Dame Law School* 269

Mario Cuomo, governor of New York, holds that freedom demands that citizens be granted the right to choose on such a complex and divisive an issue as abortion and that legal prohibitions could not succeed. Illinois Representative Henry Hyde insists that those who oppose abortion as morally wrong, including church leaders, have a right and responsibility to create a consensus against it.

ISSUE 17. Should We Have a "Wall of Separation" Between Church
and State? 276

YES: Edd Doerr, from "Does Religion Belong in Our Public Schools?"
USA Today Magazine (Society for the Advancement of Education) 278

NO: George Goldberg, from *Reconsecrating America* 285

Edd Doerr, executive director of Americans for Religious Liberty, believes that public schools, like other public institutions, should promote and reflect shared values, leaving religious instruction and celebration to the home and place of worship. George Goldberg, a writer and lawyer, holds that government may not favor one religion over another but school prayer and the

teaching of religion are permissible as long as all religions are accorded equal treatment.

ISSUE 18. Is American Intervention in Latin America Justified?   296

YES: Mark Falcoff, from "Making Central America Safe for Communism," *Commentary*   298

NO: Abraham F. Lowenthal, from "Rethinking U.S. Interests in the Western Hemisphere," *Journal of Interamerican Studies*   308

Policy analyst Mark Falcoff predicts a communist victory in Central America unless the United States takes a more active role in helping to stop Soviet penetration. Professor Abraham Lowenthal contends that the United States should focus on the economic growth and political health of Latin America as a whole instead of being obsessed with the military security of Central America.

ISSUE 19. Is the End of the Cold War in Sight?   318

YES: John Lewis Gaddis, from "How the Cold War Might End," *Atlantic Monthly*   320

NO: Richard Nixon, from "Dealing with Gorbachev," *New York Times Magazine*   331

Historian John Gaddis argues that it is no longer utopian imagining to foresee an end to the cold war. Former president Richard Nixon warns America that, if it seeks peace without victory, it is doomed to defeat.

ISSUE 20. Is America Declining?   342

YES: Paul Kennedy, from *The Rise and Fall of the Great Powers*   344

NO: W. W. Rostow, from "Beware of Historians Bearing False Analogies," *Foreign Affairs*   353

Historian Paul Kennedy believes that the United States, like other great powers before it, has developed an imbalance between international military commitments and domestic economic development, which will inevitably result in America's decline in power. W. W. Rostow, an economist and educator, maintains that Kennedy misinterprets America's balance-of-power strategy and that the United States can continue to play a leading role in international politics.

PSYCHOLOGICAL ISSUES,
Fifth Edition

ISSUE 1. Can Deception in Research Be Justified?   2

YES: Stanley Milgram, from "Subject Reaction: The Neglected Factor in the Ethics of Experimentation," *Hastings Center Report*   4

NO: Thomas H. Murray, from "Learning to Deceive," *Hastings Center Report*   13

Some researchers contend that subjects must sometimes be "fooled" into yielding important experimental results. It is argued that the results will be unreliable if the subjects know the true objective of the experiment. Is the danger of embarrassment or even anguish for the subject justified by the information that is produced?

ISSUE 2. Can Experiments Using Animals Be Justified?   22

YES: Frederick A. King, from "Animals in Research: The Case for Experimentation," *Psychology Today*   24

NO: Peter Singer, from "Tools for Research, or What the Public Doesn't Know It Is Paying For," *The New York Review of Books*   32

Psychologist Frederick King argues that psychological research using animals benefits society in many positive ways and that high standards of humane treatment are maintained. But philosopher Peter Singer describes the "brutal consequences" of animal research.

ISSUE 3. Is Our Behavior Primarily Determined by Biological Processes?   38

YES: Richard Restak, from "Is Free Will a Fraud?" *Science Digest*   40

NO: Joseph F. Rychlak, from "Free Will: 'Doing Otherwise, All Circumstances Remaining the Same,' " *an original essay written for this volume*   47

Is free will a delusion? Do biological processes control our behavior? Or does physiological research generally support the existence of free will? These

questions are addressed and debated by a forensic neurologist and a humanistic psychologist.

ISSUE 4. Do Attitudes Affect Cancer?   52

YES: Judith Glassman, from "Beating the Odds," *New Age Journal*   54

NO: Marcia Angell, from "Disease as a Reflection of the Psyche," *New England Journal of Medicine*   62

There is great trauma that attends serious disease. Can a positive attitude affect the progress of illness, or are we doing a disservice to patients by suggesting that they bear a responsibility for their condition? Science has produced conflicting evidence in response to this question.

ISSUE 5. Has Science Discredited ESP?   70

YES: C. E. M. Hansel, from *ESP and Parapsychology: A Critical Reevaluation*   72

NO: David Loye, from *The Sphinx and the Rainbow*   81

The existence of extrasensory perception has long been the subject of great debate among scientists. Has science succeeded in proving or disproving this phenomenon? Much of the debate is centered on the reliability of experimental results and how they are interpreted.

ISSUE 6. Is the State of Hypnosis a Unique Altered State of Consciousness?   88

YES: Ernest R. Hilgard, from "Hypnosis Is No Mirage," *Psychology Today*   90

NO: Theodore X. Barber, from "Who Believes in Hypnosis?" *Psychology Today*   96

In recent years, many psychologists have turned their interest inwards to the nature of mental phenomena. Concern for special states of consciousness induced by drugs, meditation, sleep, and hypnosis has raised questions about their very existence. Are they distinct and unique, or do they merely emphasize the varieties that a single state of consciousness may assume?

ISSUE 7. Should Use of the Principles of Conditioning Be Limited in the Modification of Undesirable Behavior?   106

YES: R. Joseph Lucero, David J. Vail, and John Scherber, from "Regulating Operant Conditioning," *Hospital and Community Psychology*   108

NO: Nathan B. Miron, from "Issues and Implications of Operant Conditioning," *Hospital and Community Psychology*   110

Operant conditioning principles are widely used to treat all types of problems, from student misbehavior to patient psychosis. Many have questioned their use, contending that their application is unethical and dehumanizing. A special concern is the application of conditioning to patients in mental institutions.

ISSUE 8. Can Computers Think?   116

YES: H. A. Simon, from "Using Cognitive Science to Solve Human Problems," *Science and Public Policy Seminar*   118

NO: Ulric Neisser, from "Computers Can't Think," *Creative Computing*   123

What is the nature of human thought? If machines can perform problem-solving and decision-making functions, does that make them capable of thought as we understand it? This issue goes to the very heart of our view of ourselves as unique in our reasoning abilities.

ISSUE 9. Should Children Learn Morality Primarily by Examining Their Own Reasoning?   134

YES: Lawrence Kohlberg, from "The Cognitive-Developmental Approach to Moral Education," *Phi Delta Kappan*   136

NO: Edward A. Wynne, from "The Great Tradition in Education: Transmitting Moral Values," *Educational Leadership*   145

Kohlberg discusses theories of cognitive and moral growth. He argues that moral and civic education have much in common and are most effective when educational methods are designed to stimulate personal growth. But Edward Wynne traces and provides justification for traditional methods of transmitting moral values in our educational systems.

ISSUE 10. Should Parents Provide Academic Instruction for Their Children Before They're Old Enough for School? 154

YES: Siegfried and Therese Englemann, from *Give Your Child a Superior Mind* 156

NO: David Elkind, from "Formal Education and Early Childhood Education: An Essential Difference," *Phi Delta Kappan* 163

Siegfried and Therese Engelmann claim that preschool instruction using their procedures is pleasurable and will give children a lasting head start. David Elkind forcefully argues against giving academic instruction to very young children because of the risks it can pose to a child's development.

ISSUE 11. Can Intelligence Be Increased? 174

YES: R. J. Sternberg, from "How Can We Teach Intelligence?" *Educational Leadership* 176

NO: Arthur R. Jensen, from "Compensatory Education and the Theory of Intelligence," *Educational Leadership* 187

Psychologists have long debated the origins of intelligence. Is a person's intelligence set for life, or is it possible to increase intelligence through training programs? The answers to this issue have profound educational and social implications and bring into question many long-standing assumptions.

ISSUE 12. Can Intelligence Be Measured with a Single Score? 196

YES: Arthur R. Jensen, from *Straight Talk About Mental Tests* 198

NO: Howard Gardner and James Ellison, from "The Seven Frames of Mind," *Psychology Today* 209

Is intelligence a single, measurable characteristic, or is it the result of an interaction among many elements? If the tests now in use are based on a single definition, are we making accurate assessments of intelligence or are we only predicting success or failure in school? The answers to this debate have profound social implications.

ISSUE 13. Do Diagnostic Labels Hinder the Effective Treatment of Persons with Mental Disorders? 218

YES: D.L. Rosenhan, from "On Being Sane in Insane Places," *Science* 220

NO: **Robert L. Spitzer,** from "On Pseudoscience in Science, Logic in Remission and Psychiatric Diagnosis: A Critique of 'On Being Sane in Insane Places,' " *Journal of Abnormal Psychology*   235

The traditional first step in treating a disorder is to diagnose it—that is, to classify it, give it a name, label it. But once a label has been affixed, it may put blinders on the way the problem is seen—properly or improperly.

ISSUE 14. Can Suicide Be Rational?   250

YES: **Mary Rose Barrington,** from "Apologia for Suicide," in *Suicide: The Ethical Issues*   252

NO: **Herbert Hendin,** from "The Right to Suicide," *Suicide in America*   260

We often think of suicide as a final act of desperation undertaken by a person who must be emotionally unbalanced even to contemplate such an act. Aren't there times when suicide may be the most rational way out of an intolerable situation?

ISSUE 15. Is Psychotherapy Effective?   268

YES: **Julian Meltzoff and Melvin Kornreich,** from "It Works," *Psychology Today*   270

NO: **Martin Gross,** from *The Psychological Society*   277

Treatment for psychological problems is almost as common nowadays as is treatment for physical problems. No longer is psychotherapy used exclusively for patients in mental institutions. Now, people with all types of problems are going to therapists. Are these people wasting their time and money in therapy, or are they getting significant benefits they cannot gain anywhere else?

ISSUE 16. Should Electroshock Therapy Be Discontinued?   288

YES: **Leonard Roy Frank,** from "Electroshock: A Paradigm of Psychiatric Tyranny," *Issues in Radical Therapy*   290

NO: **Harold Sackheim,** from "The Case for ECT," *Psychology Today*   297

Electroshock therapy has long been used to aid in the treatment of various emotional disturbances. Is it an unwarranted and dangerous infringement on the rights and well-being of patients, or is it a valuable and effective therapy that can produce positive results?

ISSUE 17. Is Pornography Harmful?   **306**

YES: James C. Dobson, from *Final Report of the Attorney General's Commission on Pornography*   **308**

NO: Larry Baron, Barbara Ehrenreich et al., from "Statements of the Shadow Commissioners," *The United States vs. Sex: How the Meese Commision Lied About Sex*   **315**

Psychologist James Dobson, who was a member of the Meese commission on pornography, feels that pornography is devastating to its victims. Baron, Ehrenreich, and other "Shadow Commissioners," a group of citizens concerned about the report, contend that there is no evidence to support a causal connection between pornography and possible harms.

ISSUE 18. Should Insanity be Considered a Legal Defense for Criminals?   **326**

YES: Richard Bonnie, from Statement Submitted to the Committee on the Judiciary, *United States Senate*   **328**

NO: Jonathan Rowe, from "Why Liberals Should Hate the Insanity Defense," *Washington Monthly*   **335**

Richard Bonnie has testified that a modified form of the existing insanity defense is essential because some people with mental disorders do not deserve to be punished. Jonathan Rowe feels that the insanity defense is simply, most often, a legal ploy exploited to service white, upper-middle-class defendants.

ISSUE 19. Is the Control of Human Behavior a Proper Goal for Psychology?   **346**

YES: B. F. Skinner, from "Some Issues Concerning the Control of Human Behavior: A Symposium," *Science*   **348**

NO: Carl R. Rogers, from "Some Issues Concerning the Control of Human Behavior: A Symposium," *Science*   **356**

Both behaviorism and humanism have provided strong influences in psychology. These influences have, in fact, often conflicted. One of the classic conflicts has to do with the proper overall objectives of psychology.

SOCIAL ISSUES,
Fifth Edition

Issue 1. Is It Wrong to "Politicize" Sociology?   **2**

YES: Irving Louis Horowitz, from "Disenthralling Sociology," *Society*   **4**

NO: Alvin Gouldner, from "Anti-Minotaur: The Myth of a
Value-Free Sociology," *Social Problems*   **11**

Sociologist Irving Louis Horowitz complains that sociology has become politicized and that the work of many sociologists promotes views that make social life less humane. Alvin Gouldner counters that it is impossible and, furthermore, undesirable to eliminate all value judgments from the study of society.

Issue 2. Does "Lower-Class" Culture Perpetuate Poverty?   **20**

YES: Edward Banfield, from *The Unheavenly City Revisited*   **22**

NO: William Ryan, from *Blaming the Victim*   **27**

Professor Edward Banfield suggests that it is the cultural outlook of the poor that tends to keep them in poverty. Psychologist Ryan responds that this view is a form of "blaming the victim."

Issue 3. Has Individualism Become Excessive?   **36**

YES: Robert N. Bellah et al., from *Habits of the Heart: Individualism and Commitment in American Life*   **38**

NO: Henry Fairlie, from *The Spoiled Child of the Western World: The Miscarriage of the American Idea in Our Time*   **49**

Robert Bellah and his associates argue that Americans have become self-absorbed at the expense of transcendent values and the good of the community. Henry Fairlie suggests that such criticism fails to appreciate the extraordinary degree of freedom enjoyed by modern "mass man."

Issue 4. Is Urban Life Crazy?   **56**

YES: Henry Fairlie, from "The Idiocy of Urban Life," *The New Republic*   **58**

NO: C. R. Creekmore, from "Cities Won't Drive You Crazy," *Psychology Today*   **64**

Henry Fairlie, a frequent commentator on the social scene, points out that most people flee cities whenever possible, and he enumerates the nuisances that create the exodus. C. R. Creekmore uses research findings to show that much of the criticisms of urban life is based on myths and is unfounded.

Issue 5. Are Traditional Families More Successful?   **74**

YES: Phyllis Schlafly, from *The Power of the Positive Woman*   **76**

NO: Barbara Deckard, from *The Women's Movement: Political, Socio-economic and Psychological Issues,* Second Edition   **83**

Conservative activist Phyllis Schlafly supports the traditional role of wife and mother as the source of fulfillment for women. Sociologist Barbara Deckard suggests that this role is demeaning and limiting and unvalued in our society.

Issue 6. Can Women Combine Careers and Families?   **92**

YES: Shirley Wilkins and Thomas A.W. Miller, from "Working Women: How It's Working Out," *Public Opinion*   **94**

NO: George Gilder, from "Women in the Work Force," *Atlantic Monthly*   **102**

Basing their remarks on a national survey, Shirley Wilkins and Thomas Miller show that most women want to combine work and family even though it may be difficult. Sociologist George Gilder argues that women are much less committed to careers than men, and he uses various data to support his conclusions.

Issue 7. The "New Woman": Has She Confused Sex Roles?   **108**

YES: Donald Singletary, from "You New Women Want it Both Ways!" *Essence*   **110**

NO: Betty Winston Baye, from "You Men Want It All!" *Essence*   **116**

Donald Singletary accuses modern young women of "wanting it both ways" (i.e., they want the advantages of liberation and the advantages that come with more traditional roles). Betty Winston Baye makes the arguement that men say they want educated, independent, money-making women, but their egos cannot handle a true equal.

Issue 8. Is Economic Inequality Beneficial to Society?   **122**

YES: George Gilder, from *Wealth and Poverty*   **124**

NO: William Ryan, from *Equality*   **136**

Sociologist George Gilder praises the American political economy that provides so many incentives for people to get ahead and make money, and claims that the economy is dynamic and that all classes benefit from it. Psychologist William Ryan contends that income inequalities in America are excessive and immoral because they vastly exceed differences of merit and result in tremendous hardships for the poor.

Issue 9. Is Racial Oppression Declining in America?   **148**

YES: William J. Wilson, from *The Declining Significance of Race*   **150**

NO: Charles V. Willie, from "The Inclining Significance of Race,"
Society   **158**

Sociologist William J. Wilson argues that class, rather than race, is now the dominant factor in determining a person's life chances. Educator Charles V. Willie counters that race remains the primary consideration.

Issue 10. Is Affirmative Action Reverse Discrimination?   **164**

YES: Glenn C. Loury, from "Beyond Civil Rights," *The New Republic*   **166**

NO: Herman Schwartz, from "In Defense of Affirmative Action,"
Dissent   **173**

Harvard professor Glenn Loury contends that insistence on "ill-suited" civil rights strategies makes it impossible for blacks to achieve full equality in American society. Professor Herman Schwartz argues that we must somehow undo the cruel consequences of racism that still plague our society and its victims.

Issue 11. Does an Elite Rule America?   **182**

YES: G. William Domhoff, from *Who Rules America Now?: A View
for the '80s*   **184**

NO: Andrew Greeley, from *Building Coalitions: American Politics in the
1970s*   **194**

Sociologist G. William Domhoff tries to demonstrate that the American upperclass occupies a surprisingly large number of influential positions in society which enables it to rule America. Sociologist Andrew M. Greeley argues that there is no single established center of power and points to the behavior of the system as evidence to support his view.

Issue 12. Has American Government Gotten Too Big?   200

YES: William Simon, from *A Time for Truth*   202

NO: John Kenneth Galbraith, from "The Social Consensus and the
Conservative Onslaught," *The Millenium Journal of International Studies* **208**

Former Treasury Secretary William Simon argues that excessive government
involvement in the economy abridges basic liberties and hurts the nation's
productivity. Economist John Kenneth Galbraith says that since public
services are essential to those Americans who can't afford private services,
the attack on "big government" is really an attack on the poor.

Issue 13. Does Welfare Do More Harm Than Good?   214

YES: Charles Murray, from *Losing Ground*   216

NO: Christopher Jencks, from "How Poor Are the Poor?" *The New
York Review of Books*   226

Charles Murray outlines his contention that welfare programs can result in
long-term dependency on the part of the poor. Social commentator Christopher Jencks argues that government aid programs are vital to meeting the
needs of the poor.

Issue 14. Are Homosexual Relations Deviant?   238

YES: Robert Gordis, from "Homosexuality and the Homosexual,"
Homosexuality and Ethics   240

NO: Jeannine Gramick, from an essay written for *Taking Sides:
Clashing Views on Controversial Issues in Human Sexuality*   248

Robert Gordis, a biblical professor at the Jewish Theological Seminary, argues
that homosexuality is contrary to the natural sexual programming of the
human species and should be considered and treated as an illness or
abnormality. Jeannine Gramick, who ministers to homosexuals, argues that
homosexuality is natural and normal and may be genetically determined.
She supports her view by reviewing the prevalence of homosexuality in
history.

Issue 15. Is Incapacitation the Answer to the Crime Problem?   258

YES: James Q. Wilson, from *Thinking About Crime*   260

NO: David Bazelon, from "Solving the Nightmare of Street Crime,"
USA Today Magazine   273

Professor James Q. Wilson argues that imprisoning everyone convicted of a serious crime for several years would greatly reduce these crimes. He contends that incapacitation is the one policy that works. Judge David L. Bazelon discusses the moral and financial costs of the incapacitation approach and argues that society must attack the brutal social and economic conditions that are the root causes of street crime.

Issue 16. Should Immigration Be More Limited?   282

YES: Gary Imhoff, from "Sovereignty and Security: Immigration Today," *The Humanist*   284

NO: Julian L. Simon, from "Don't Close Our Border," *Newsweek*   290

Gary Imhoff looks at the recent figures on immigration and argues that excessive immigration poses serious dangers to Americans and undermines the sovereignty of the nation. Economist and social commentator Julian Simon contends that immigration invigorates and enriches America.

Issue 17. Is Nuclear Deterrence Irrational?   294

YES: Jonathan Schell, from *The Fate of the Earth*   296

NO: Charles Krauthammer, from "The Real Way to Prevent Nuclear War," *The New Republic*   305

In arguing for an end to the nuclear arms race, Jonathan Schell, staff writer for the *New Yorker*, explores the consequences of nuclear war and its implications for the human race and the earth itself. Charles Krauthammer, senior editor of the *New Republic*, does not dispute the terror of nuclear war, but he argues that this very balance of terror is what prevents war from occurring.

Issue 18. Is the World Threatened by a Population Bomb?   316

YES: Steven Mumford, from "Population Growth and Global Security," *The Humanist*   318

NO: Julian L. Simon, from "World Population Growth," *The Atlantic Monthly*   323

Steven Mumford, an expert in population studies, makes his case that population over-growth is the most serious threat to our lives and security. Economist Julian Simon defends his optimistic view that increased population will make greater opportunities available to future generations.

Issue 19. Is the Environment Improving?   330

YES: Julian L. Simon, from "Life on Earth Is Getting Better, Not
Worse," *The Futurist*   332

NO: Lester R. Brown and Sandra L. Postel, from "Thresholds of
Change," *The Futurist*   338

Economist Julian Simon reviews several indicators of improving environmental conditions for human life. Lester Brown and Sandra Postel, from the
Worldwatch Institute, argue that many of the earth's natural systems have
become seriously destabilized in environmentally destructive ways.

Issue 20. Is America Headed for an Economic Bust?   346

YES: Richard D. Lamm, from *Megatraumas: America at the Year 2000*   348

NO: Marshall Loeb, from "The Economy of 1987—and Beyond," *Vital
Speeches of the Day*   354

Former governor of Colorado Richard Lamm sees America headed into an
era of economic crisis brought on by reckless spending and inadequate
investment. Marshall Loeb of *Fortune* magazine predicts that America is
entering a prolonged period of economic growth.

WORLD POLITICS,
Second Edition

ISSUE 1. Is the United States Becoming Too Friendly with China?   **2**

YES: Ray S. Cline, from "China's Conversion: Cause for Concern," *The World & I*   **4**

NO: Donald Zagoria, from Statement to U.S. Congress, House Committee on Foreign Affairs, *United States-China Relations*   **9**

Ray Cline, who is currently at the Center for Strategic and International Studies, Georgetown University, and who was formerly deputy director of the Central Intelligence Agency, argues that the United States is making a mistake by trying to become friendly with a still-communist China. Donald Zagoria, professor of government at Hunter College and City University of New York, contends that China has undertaken substantial reform and that it is in the strategic interest of the United States to befriend China.

ISSUE 2. Do U.S. Allies Share the Defense Burden Fairly?   **16**

YES: Michael Legge, from "The View from London," *The National Interest*   **18**

NO: Richard Perle, from ". . . And from Washington," *The National Interest*   **26**

Michael Legge, who is assistant under-secretary for policy at the British Ministry of Defense, argues that Europe makes many contributions to NATO beyond financial ones, which balances U.S. financial contributions. Richard Perle, a resident scholar at the American Enterprise Institute and former U.S. assistant secretary of defense for international security policy, writes that prosperous U.S. allies should contribute more to NATO and should give the U.S. greater support globally.

ISSUE 3. Is U.S. Intervention in Latin America and Elsewhere Justified?   **34**

YES: Charles Krauthammer, from "Guerrilla Warfare: Morality and the Reagan Doctrine," *The New Republic*   **36**

NO: Michael Parenti, from *The Sword and the Dollar*   **46**

Charles Krauthammer, a political commentator, argues in favor of U.S. interventionism as a policy that is morally and pragmatically justifiable. Michael Parenti, a former political science professor and currently an independent academic analyst, denounces both liberal and conservative supported interventions as examples of U.S. imperialism.

ISSUE 4. Should Strict Sanctions Be Applied Against South Africa?   56

YES: Robert G. Mugabe, from "Struggle for Southern Africa," *Foreign Affairs*   58

NO: John C. Whitehead, from "The Potential Impact of Imposing Sanctions Against South Africa," *Department of State Bulletin*   66

Robert Mugabe, prime minister of Zimbabwe, contends that the United States and other countries should impose strict economic sanctions on South Africa in order to force its government to end apartheid. John Whitehead, U.S. deputy secretary of state, argues that South Africa is easing apartheid and that strict sanctions will be counterproductive and will economically injure South African blacks.

ISSUE 5. Should Israel Agree to the Creation of a Palestinian State?   76

YES: Yehoshafat Harkabi, from "A Policy for the Moment of Truth," *Jerusalem Post International Edition*   78

NO: David Bar-Illan, from "Can Israel Withdraw? No!" *Commentary*   86

Yehoshafat Harkabi, professor of international relations at Hebrew University in Jerusalem and former head of Israeli military intelligence, argues that Israel is facing a moment of truth and that, while an independent Palestine is not a good choice, it is the best one given the alternatives. David Bar-Illan, director of the Jonathan Institute, an antiterrorist organization headquartered in Jerusalem, also sees Israel's choices ranging from bad to worse, but he holds that an independent Palestine would present an even greater threat to Israel that the current situation.

ISSUE 6. Does the Soviet Union Truly Want International Co-operation?   96

YES: Mikhail S. Gorbachev, from *Perestroika*   98

NO: Alain Besançon, from "Gorbachev Without Illusions," *Commentary*   107

Soviet general secretary Gorbachev says he seeks true international cooperation to avoid potential military, economic, and environmental disaster.
French commentator Besançon, a professor at the Ecole des Hautes Etudes in
Paris, believes that the Soviet Union remains a dangerous opponent and that
perestroika is deluding the West.

ISSUE 7. Is the United States a Declining Power?   122

YES: Paul Kennedy, from "The (Relative) Decline of America," *The Atlantic Monthly*   124

NO: Owen Harries, from "The Rise of American Decline," *Commentary*   133

Paul Kennedy, the J. Richardson Dilworth professor of history at Yale
University, argues that the United States is militarily overextended, a condition which is sapping its economic strength and speeding its relative decline
in power. Diplomat Owen Harries, former head of policy planning, Australian Department of Foreign Affairs, contends that the United States is not
overextended and that Kennedy's analysis is flawed.

ISSUE 8. Will the Canada-U.S. Free Trade Agreement Be Beneficial?   142

YES: Brian Mulroney, from the Canadian House of Commons *Debates*   144

NO: John N. Turner, from the Canadian House of Commons *Debates*   154

Prime minister of Canada Brian Mulroney supports the free trade treaty
between Canada and the United States as economically beneficial. John
Turner, leader of Canada's Liberal Party and former prime minister, attacks
Mulroney for putting Canada "up for sale" by agreeing to the free trade
treaty.

ISSUE 9. Do Foreign Investments Threaten U.S. Economic Independence?   166

YES: Martin and Susan Tolchin, from *Buying into America: How Foreign Money Is Changing the Face of the Nation*   168

NO: Grover Norquist, from "Investing in Success," *The World & I*   176

Martin Tolchin, a reporter for the *New York Times*, and Susan Tolchin, a
professor at George Washington University, argue that foreign investors are

gaining control of too many U.S. economic resources, which threatens the country's economic and political independence. Grover Norquist, president of Americans for Tax Reform, rejects the Tolchins' analysis and says that foreign investment is a natural part of increased economic ties, is too limited to threaten U.S. independence, and is often beneficial.

**ISSUE 10. Is the Third World Responsible for Its Own Lack of
Economic Development?**   **184**

YES: Thomas Sowell, from "Second Thoughts About the Third World,"
Harper's   **186**

NO: Michael Manley, from "We Are Told . . . We Must Have More
of the Disease," *Harper's*   **195**

Thomas Sowell, a fellow at the Hoover Institution, Stanford University, contends that much of the poverty in the Third World results from governments there that repress, impede, or even drive out those who are capable of aiding development. Michael Manley, the recently elected prime minister of Jamaica, replies that imperialism subjugated the Third World and continues to keep it underdeveloped.

**ISSUE 11. Should the Less Developed Countries Pay Their
International Debts?**   **202**

YES: Jack D. Guenther, from U.S. Congress, House Committee on
Banking, Finance and Urban Affairs, *Third World Debt*   **204**

NO: Julio Silva Colmenares, from "Deeper Contradictions Between
Latin America and Imperialism," *World Marxist Review*   **211**

U.S. banker Jack Guenther, who is senior vice president for International Operations for Citibank, maintains that payment of the Third World's debt will benefit both Third World countries and their creditors. Julio Silva Colmenares, a member of Columbia's Communist Party, says Third World debt is imperialistic and that the Third World countries should refuse to pay it.

**ISSUE 12. Could NATO Forces Withstand a Conventional Attack by
the Warsaw Pact?**   **222**

YES: John Mearsheimer, from U.S. Congress, Senate Committee on
Armed Services, *Alliance and Defense Capabilities in Europe*   **224**

NO: Eliot A. Cohen, from U.S. Congress, Senate Committee on Armed Services, *Alliance and Defense Capabilities in Europe*   **231**

John Mearsheimer, professor of political science at the University of Chicago, says that despite the Warsaw Pact's numerical advantage, NATO has a 7 in 10 chance of defeating an attack. U.S. Naval War College analyst Cohen argues that a Warsaw Pact attack probably would overwhelm NATO defenses.

ISSUE 13. Should Superpower Strategic Arsenals Be Cut in Half?   **240**

YES: John B. Ritch III and James P. Rubin, from "Arms Control—Now or Never," *Bulletin of the Atomic Scientists*   **242**

NO: Patrick Glynn, from "Reagan's Rush to Disarm," *Commentary*   **250**

John Ritch, deputy director of the U.S. Senate Committee on Foreign Relations, and James Rubin, assistant director of the Arms Control Association, contend that cutting the superpowers' strategic arsenals in half will reduce the chance of nuclear war and have other benefits as well. Patrick Glynn, a resident scholar at the American Enterprise Institute and former special assistant to the director of the U.S. Arms Control and Disarmament Agency, believes that a 50% strategic nuclear weapons reduction will increase U.S. vulnerability to a Soviet attack, thereby increasing the chance of nuclear war.

ISSUE 14. Can Military Action Reduce International Terrorism?   **260**

YES: Benjamin Netanyahu, from "Terrorism: How the West Can Win" *Time*   **262**

NO: Martha Crenshaw, from "Terrorism: What Shall We Do?" in Steven Anzovin, ed., *Terrorism*   **269**

Benjamin Netanyahu, former Israeli ambassador to the United Nations, says military action can deter terrorism and cites Israel's experience to prove it. Martha Crenshaw, professor of government at Wesleyan University, argues that military responses to terrorism are ineffective and give terrorists the status and publicity they desire.

ISSUE 15. Should Morality and Human Rights Strongly Influence Foreign Policymaking?   **278**

YES: Cyrus Vance, from "The Human Rights Imperative," *Foreign Policy*   **280**

NO: George Schultz, from "Morality and Realism in American Foreign Policy," *Department of State Bulletin*   288

Former U.S. secretary of state Vance contends that a commitment to human rights must be a central principle of foreign policy. Former U.S. secretary of state George Shultz argues that foreign policy must avoid idealism if it conflicts with the national interest.

ISSUE 16. Should the U.S. Congress Limit the President's War Powers?   294

YES: Lowell Weicker, from address to the Senate, *Congressional Record*   296

NO: J. Danforth Quayle, from address to the Senate, *Congressional Record*   302

Lowell Weicker, former Republican senator from Connecticut, maintains that the Constitution and democratic principles mandate congressional participation in decisions to commit U.S. military forces to war or situations where war might occur. Dan Quayle, former Republican senator from Indiana and current U.S. vice president, says the War Powers Resolution unwisely restricts the president's necessary and constitutional ability to act decisively.

ISSUE 17. International Law: Should the United States Expel the PLO's Mission to the United Nations?   310

YES: Charles Grassley, from address to the Senate, *Congressional Record*   312

NO: Achmet Ansay, from address to the U.N. General Assembly, *Provisional Verbatim Record*   315

U.S. senator Charles Grassley (R-Iowa) condemns the PLO as a terrorist organization and wants its observer mission to the United Nations expelled from New York City. Ambassador Ansay, representing the Organization of the Islamic Conference's mission to the United Nations, argues that expelling the PLO mission would violate the U.S.-U.N. headquarters agreement and international law.

ISSUE 18. Is the United Nations a Beneficial Organization?   320

YES: C. R. Gharekhan, from "Imagine a World Without It," *The World & I*   322

NO: Tom Bethell, from "The Last Best Hope at Forty," *National Review*   **328**

India's ambassador to the United Nations Gharekhan argues that while the United Nations has not fulfilled everyone's expectations, it has accomplished much, and the world is better off with it. Tom Bethell, fellow at the Hoover Institute at Stanford University, says the United Nations is ineffective and primarily serves as a forum for criticism of the United States.

ISSUE 19. Is the World Climate Threatened by Global Warming?   **334**

YES: David J. Rose, Marvin M. Miller, and Carson Agnew, from "Reducing the Problem of Global Warming," *Technology Review*   **336**

NO: Tom Yulsman, from "Greenhouse Earth," *Science Digest*   **345**

David Rose, professor of nuclear engineering at Massachusetts Institute of Technology, Marvin Miller, research scientist at Massachusetts Institute of Technology, and Carson Agnew, engineering economist with Hughes Aircraft Corporation, say the Earth is threatened by an increase in temperature and urge immediate world cooperation to reduce the effects of the warming climate. Tom Yulsman, news editor of *Science Digest*, questions the methodology of those predicting significant warming and argues that there is no need for urgent action.

Issue List

ISSUE LIST

Sample Entry	Explanatory Note
Do Political Action ①	① issue
Committees	② *Taking Sides*
Undermine ②	volume in which
Democracy? *Pol,*	issue appears
Issue 3 ③	(abbreviation)
	③ issue number
	within *Taking*
	Sides volume

— A —

Abortion: Should Public Officials Protect the "Right to Choose"? *Pol,* Issue 16

Are Abundant Resources and an Improved Environment Likely Future Prospects for the World's People? *Env,* Issue 19

Are Environmentalists and Industrial Leaders Becoming Less Adversarial? *Env,* Issue 5

Are Homosexual and Bisexual Relations Natural and Normal? *HS,* Issue 3

Are Homosexual Relations Deviant? *Soc,* Issue 14

Are Official Statistics Meaningful? *CR,* Issue 5

Are Packaged Discipline Programs Harmful? *Edu,* Issue 16

Are Profits the Only Business of Business? *Mor,* Issue 15, *Eco,* Issue 1

Are Proposed Elementary School Reforms Realistic? *Edu,* Issue 11

Are School-Based Health Clinics an Effective Way of Reducing Teenage Pregnancies and STDs? *HS,* Issue 8

Are Specific Programs to Teach Thinking Needed? *Edu,* Issue 13

Are Tests of Teacher Knowledge Fair? *Edu,* Issue 20

Are the Cards Stacked Against True School Reform? *Edu,* Issue 9

Are There Limits to Confidentiality? *Bio,* Issue 8

Are There Too Many Hostile Takeovers? *Eco,* Issue 5

Are Traditional Families More Successful? *Soc,* Issue 5

— C —

Can Computers Think? *Psy,* Issue 8

Can Deception in Psychological Research Be Justified? *Psy,* Issue 1

Can Deception in Research Be Justified? *Bio,* Issue 11

Can Experiments Using Animals Be Justified? *Psy,* Issue 2

Can Federal Budget Deficits Be Good for the Economy? *Eco,* Issue 14

Can Intelligence Be Increased? *Psy,* Issue 11

Can Intelligence Be Measured with a Single Score? *Psy,* Issue 12

Can Military Action Reduce International Terrorism? *WP,* Issue 14

Can Monetary and Fiscal Policies Still Be Used to Solve Our Macroeconomic Problems? *Eco,* Issue 11

Can Sex Be an Addiction? *HS,* Issue 6

Can Suicide Be Rational? *Psy,* Issue 14

Can the Revolution Serve as a Developmental Model for Third World Nations Today? *AH1,* Issue 6

Can Women Combine Careers and Families? *Soc,* Issue 6

Constitution, The: Was It an Economic Document? *AH1,* Issue 7

Could NATO Forces Withstand a Conventional Attack by the Warsaw Pact? *WP,* Issue 12

Could the United States Have Prevented the Fall of South Vietnam? *AH2,* Issue 14

— D —

Did American Slaves Develop a Distinct Afro-American Culture in the Eighteenth Century? *AH1,* Issue 4

Did Monetary Policy Cause the Stock Market Crash in 1987? *Eco,* Issue 15

Did President Jefferson Outfederalize the Federalists? *AH1*, Issue 8

Did Slavery Destroy the Black Family? *AH1*, Issue 13

Did the Election of 1828 Represent a Democratic Revolt of the People? *AH1*, Issue 10

Did the Progressives Fail? *AH2*, Issue 7

Did the Women's Movement Die in the 1920s? *AH2*, Issue 10

Did Women Achieve Greater Autonomy in the New Nation? *AH1*, Issue 9

Did Woodrow Wilson Fail as Commander-in-Chief During World War II? *AH2*, Issue 9

Do Attitudes Affect Cancer? *Psy*, Issue 4

Do Diagnostic Labels Hinder the Effective Treatment of Persons with Mental Disorders? *Psy*, Issue 13

Does an Elite Rule America? *Soc*, Issue 11

Does Behavioral Control Provide the Best Learning Environment? *Edu*, Issue 6

Does Drug Use Testing Violate the Fourth Amendment? *Leg*, Issue 6

Does Good Sex Require Love? *HS*, Issue 4

Does Government Have a Constitutional Right to Prohibit Certain Kinds of Sexual Conduct? *HS*, Issue 14

Does Government Have a Right to Prohibit Homosexual Acts? *Pol*, Issue 15

Does "Lower Class" Culture Perpetuate Poverty? *Soc*, Issue 2

Does Morality Require Nuclear Disarmament? *Mor*, Issue 18

Does Our Welfare System Hurt the Poor? *Pol*, Issue 14

Does Pornography Promote Sexual Violence? *HS*, Issue 13

Does Risk-Benefit Analysis Provide an Objective Method for Making Environmental Decisions? *Env*, Issue 4

Does Society Have an Obligation to Care for the Less Well Off? *Mor*, Issue 16

Does the Government Regulate Too Much? *Pol*, Issue 8

Does the Montreal Ozone Agreement Signal a New Era of International Environmental Statesmanship? *Env*, Issue 18

Does the Soviet Union Truly Want International Cooperation? *WP*, Issue 6

Does the Supreme Court Abuse Its Power? *Pol*, Issue 9

Does Tracking Support Educational Inequality? *Edu*, Issue 18

Does Welfare Do More Harm Than Good? *Soc*, Issue 13

Does Wilderness Have Intrinsic Value? *Env*, Issue 1

Do Firms Exploit Workers and Local Communities by Closing Profitable Plants? *Eco*, Issue 7

Do Foreign Investments Threaten U.S. Economic Independence? *WP*, Issue 9

Do Patients Have a Right to Die? *Leg*, Issue 13

Do Political Action Committees Undermine Democracy? *Pol*, Issue 3

Do Rich Nations Have an Obligation to Help Poor Nations? *Pol*, Issue 17

Do Surrogate Motherhood Contracts Exploit Women? *HS*, Issue 18

Do the Ends Justify the Means? *Mor*, Issue 5

Do the News Media Have a Liberal Bias? *Pol*, Issue 4

Do U.S. Allies Share the Defense Burden Fairly? *WP*, Issue 2

Do We Have a Moral Responsibility to Rehabilitate Criminals? *Mor*, Issue 10

Do We Have a Moral Right to Die? *Mor*, Issue 6

Do We Need More Jails? *CR*, Issue 14

Do We Need More Stringently Enforced Regulations to Protect Endangered Species? *Env*, Issue 2

Do We Need New Federal Legislation to Protect the Future Integrity of Our Groundwater? *Env*, Issue 16

— H —

Has American Government Become Too Big? *Eco*, Issue 10

Has American Government Gotten Too Big? *Soc*, Issue 12

Has Congress Restricted Presidential War Powers Too Much? *Pol*, Issue 7

Has Individualism Become Excessive? *Soc*, Issue 3

Has Science Discredited ESP? *Psy*, Issue 5

Has the Women's Movement Increased Female Criminality? *CR*, Issue 7

Have American Political Parties Lost Their Power? *Pol*, Issue 2

Hazardous Waste: Can Present Regulatory and Voluntary Efforts Solve Disposal and Clean-Up Problems? *Env*, Issue 13

— I —

International Law: Should the United States Expel the PLO's Mission to the United Nations? *WP*, Issue 17

Is Abortion Always Immoral? *Mor*, Issue 8

Is Abortion Immoral? *Bio*, Issue 1

Is Affirmative Action Constitutional? *Leg*, Issue 11

Is Affirmative Action Morally Justifiable? *Mor*, Issue 14

Is Affirmative Action Reverse Discrimination? *Pol*, Issue 12, *Soc*, Issue 10

Is America Declining? *Pol*, Issue 20

Is America Headed for an Economic Bust? *Soc*, Issue 20

Is American Intervention in Latin America Justified? *Pol*, Issue 18

Is America Ruled by an Elite? *Pol*, Issue 1

Is Bilingual Education Justifiable as a Policy? *Edu*, Issue 19

Is Capital Punishment Justified? *Pol*, Issue 11

Is Church-State Separation Being Threatened? *Edu*, Issue 5

Is "Comparable Worth" Worthless? *Eco*, Issue 4

Is Crime Created by Society's Elites? *CR*, Issue 2

Is Crime Functional? *CR*, Issue 1

Is Crime Getting Worse? *CR*, Issue 6

Is Criminal Behavior Biologically Determined? *CR*, Issue 3

Is Economic Inequality Beneficial to Society? *Soc*, Issue 8

Is EPA's Strategy Evolving to Meet Present and Future Environmental Problems? *Env*, Issue 3

Is Euthanasia Immoral? *Mor*, Issue 7

Is Extramarital Sex Wrong? *Mor*, Issue 9

Is Genetic Engineering a Threat to Future Generations? *Bio*, Issue 20

Is Immediate Action Necessary to Minimize Potential Catastrophic Effects of Global Climatic Warming? *Env*, Issue 17

Is Immediate Legislative Action Needed to Combat the Effects of Acid Rain? *Env*, Issue 11

Is Incapacitation the Answer to the Crime Problem? *Soc*, Issue 15

Is Involuntary Commitment Wrong? *Bio*, Issue 9

Is It Ethical to Implant Animal Hearts in Humans? *Bio*, Issue 12

Is It Ethical to Withhold the Truth from Dying Patients? *Bio*, Issue 4

Is It Time to Abolish the Minimum Wage? *Eco*, Issue 9

Is It Unconstitutional to Discriminate Against Homosexuals? *Leg*, Issue 7

Is It Wrong to Create Test-tube Babies? *Bio*, Issue 2

Is It Wrong to "Politicize" Sociology? *Soc*, Issue 1

Is "Killing" the Same as "Letting Die"? *Bio*, Issue 5

Is Mainstreaming Beneficial to All? *Edu*, Issue 17

Is Manufacturing Alive and Well and Living in the U.S.? *Eco*, Issue 20

Is Measurement-Driven Instruction Desirable? *Edu*, Issue 15

Is Monogamy the Best Form of Marriage? *HS*, Issue 5

Is Morality Relative? *Mor*, Issue 1

Is Morality Subjective? *Mor*, Issue 2

Is Morality the Exclusive Province of Religion? *Mor*, Issue 3

Is Nuclear Deterrence Irrational? *Soc*, Issue 17

Is Nuclear Power Safe and Desirable? *Env,* Issue 8

Is Our Behavior Primarily Determined by Biological Processes? *Psy,* Issue 3

Is Population Control the Key to Preventing Environmental Deterioration? *Env,* Issue 6

Is Pornography a Threat to Society? *Mor,* Issue 12

Is Pornography Harmful? *Psy,* Issue 17

Is Psychotherapy Effective? *Psy,* Issue 15

Is Racial Oppression Declining in America? *Soc,* Issue 9

Is Rape Motivated by Aggression Instead of Sex? *HS,* Issue 12

Is Selective Incapacitation Just? *CR,* Issue 12

Is Sex Education in Schools an Attempt to Institutionalize a Sexual Revolution? *HS,* Issue 7

Is Street Crime More Serious Than White-Collar Crime? *CR,* Issue 4

Is Tax Reform an Impossible Dream Come True? *Eco,* Issue 12

Is the Antiabortion Movement Based on a Belief in the Sacredness of Human Life? *HS,* Issue 11

Is the Control of Human Behavior a Proper Goal for Psychology? *Psy,* Issue 19

Is the Criminal Justice System Racist? *CR,* Issue 8

Is the End of the Cold War in Sight? *Pol,* Issue 19

Is the Environment Improving? *Soc,* Issue 19

Is the Legal Profession Declining? *Leg,* Issue 5

Is the Middle Class Shrinking? *Eco,* Issue 19

Is the "New Woman" the Main Cause of Turmoil and Tension in Male/Female Relations Today? *HS,* Issue 2

Is the Pain and Suffering Associated with Disinvestment and Sanctions Worth It for Black South African Workers? *Eco,* Issue 18

Is There a Cancer Epidemic Due to Industrial Chemicals in the Environment? *Env,* Issue 10

Is There a Litigation Crisis? *Leg,* Issue 2

Is the Sexual Revolution Over? *HS,* Issue 1

Is the State of Hypnosis a Unique Altered State of Consciousness? *Psy,* Issue 6

Is the Third World Responsible for Its Own Lack of Economic Development? *WP,* Issue 10

Is the United Nations a Beneficial Organization? *WP,* Issue 18

Is the United States a Declining Power? *WP,* Issue 7

Is the United States Becoming Too Friendly with China? *WP,* Issue 1

Is the United States in a Period of Decline? *AH2,* Issue 16

Is the Victims' Rights Movement Succeeding? *CR,* Issue 18

Is the Welfare System Causing Poverty? *Eco,* Issue 13

Is the Widespread Use of Pesticides Required to Feed the World's People? *Env,* Issue 9

Is the World Climate Threatened by Global Warming? *WP,* Issue 19

Is the World Threatened by a Population Bomb? *Soc,* Issue 18

Is Urban Life Crazy? *Soc,* Issue 4

Is U.S. Intervention in Latin America and Elsewhere Justified? *WP,* Issue 3

— J —

Juvenile Justice: Are Kids "Getting Away With Murder"? *CR,* Issue 10

— M —

Municipal Waste: Is Modern Waste Incineration Technology an Environmentally Benign Alternative to Garbage Dumps? *Env,* Issue 14

Must All Students Be Given the Same Schooling? *Edu,* Issue 10

Must Fluids and Nutrition Always Be Given to Dying Patients? *Bio,* Issue 6

— N —

"New Woman," The: Has She Confused Sex Roles? *Soc*, Issue 7

Nuclear Waste: Was Yucca Mountain an Appropriate Site for Nuclear Waste Disposal? *Env*, Issue 15

— S —

Should Animal Experimentation Be Permitted? *Bio*, Issue 14

Should Capital Punishment Be Abolished? *Mor*, Issue 11, *CR*, Issue 13

Should Children Learn Morality by Examining Their Own Reasoning? *Psy*, Issue 9

Should Compulsory Schooling Be Abolished? *Edu*, Issue 7

Should Congress Be Reformed? *Pol*, Issue 5

Should Congress Guarantee U.S. Workers the Right to Parental Leave? *Eco*, Issue 8

Should Curricula Emphasize Commonality Over Diversity? *Edu*, Issue 3

Should Doctors Cut Costs at the Bedside? *Bio*, Issue 10

Should Electroshock Therapy Be Discontinued? *Psy*, Issue 16

Should Handguns Be Banned? *Leg*, Issue 16

Should Health Care for the Elderly Be Limited? *Bio*, Issue 19

Should Immigration Be More Limited? *Soc*, Issue 16

Should Insanity be Considered a Legal Defense for Criminals? *Psy*, Issue 18

Should Insurance Companies Be Allowed to Screen for Antibodies to the AIDS Virus? *Bio*, Issue 18

Should Israel Agree to the Creation of a Palestinian State? *WP*, Issue 5

Should Lawyers Use "Hardball" Tactics? *CR*, Issue 11

Should Literacy Be Based on Traditional Culture? *Edu*, Issue 14

Should Morality and Human Rights Strongly Influence Foreign Policymaking? *WP*, Issue 15

Should Newborns Without Brains Be Used as Organ Donors? *Bio*, Issue 16

Should One Always Follow One's Conscience? *Mor*, Issue 4

Should Organ Procurement Be Based on Voluntarism? *Bio*, Issue 15

Should Our Society Recognize Nonmarital and Gay Unions? *HS*, Issue 16

Should Parents Be Allowed to Decide to Withhold Treatment from Newborns with Birth Defects? *Bio*, Issue 7

Should Parents Provide Academic Instruction for Their Children Before They're Old Enough for School? *Edu*, Issue 10

Should Plea Bargaining Be Abolished? *Leg*, Issue 3

Should Pornography Be Protected by the First Amendment? *Leg*, Issue 10

Should Prayer Be Permitted in Public Schools? *Leg*, Issue 8

Should Prenatal Testing for Sex Selection Be Permitted? *HS*, Issue 9

Should Prostitution Be Decriminalized? *HS*, Issue 17

Should Regulation of Airborne Toxins Under the Clean Air Act Be Strengthened? *Env*, Issue 7

Should Research with Aborted Fetal Tissue Be Banned? *Bio*, Issue 13

Should Schooling Be Based on Students' Social Experiences? *Edu*, Issue 1

Should Schools Determine What Is Learned? *Edu*, Issue 2

Should State-Supported Family Life Education Programs Stress Premarital Chastity and Monogamy? *HS*, Issue 15

Should Strict Sanctions Be Applied Against South Africa? *WP*, Issue 4

Should Superpower Strategic Arsenals Be Cut in Half? *WP*, Issue 13

Should Surrogate Motherhood Contracts Be Illegal? *Leg*, Issue 12

Should the Adversary System Be Abolished? *Leg*, Issue 1

Should the Death Penalty Be Abolished? *Leg*, Issue 14

Should the Exclusionary Rule Be Abolished? *Leg*, Issue 15

Should the Federal Government Deregulate American Business? *Eco*, Issue 6

Should the Insanity Defense Be Abolished? *Leg*, Issue 17

Should the Law Enforce Morality? *Mor*, Issue 13

Should the Less Developed Countries Pay Their International Debts? *WP*, Issue 11

Should the Police Direct Community Crime Prevention? *CR*, Issue 9

Should the Police Do More to Manage Street Life? *Leg*, Issue 4

Should There Be a Market in Body Parts? *Bio*, Issue 17

Should There Be a Right to Abortion? *Leg*, Issue 9

Should the Schools Serve National Economic Needs? *Edu*, Issue 8

Should the U.S. Congress Limit the President's War Powers? *WP*, Issue 16

Should the U.S. Protect Domestic Industries from Foreign Competition? *Eco*, Issue 16

Should Use of the Principles of Conditioning Be Limited in the Modification of Undesirable Behavior? *Psy*, Issue 7

Should Values Be Developed Rather Than Transmitted? *Edu*, Issue 4

Should Very Young Children Receive Academic Instruction? *Edu*, Issue 12

Should We Deregulate the Blood Banking Industry? *Eco*, Issue 3

Should We Examine the Private Lives of Presidential Candidates? *Pol*, Issue 6

Should We Have a "Wall of Separation" Between Church and State? *Pol*, Issue 17

Should We Send Criminals to Penal Colonies? *CR*, Issue 16

Should We Try to Save the Family Farm? *Eco*, Issue 2

Should Women Be Allowed to Bear Babies for a Fee? *Bio*, Issue 3

Should Women Be Excluded from Jobs That Could Be Hazardous to a Fetus? *Env*, Issue 12

Should Workers Be Paid According to "Comparable Worth"? *Pol*, Issue 13

— W —

Was Abraham Lincoln America's Greatest President? *AH1*, Issue 16

Was Antebellum Reform Motivated Primarily by Humanitarian Goals? *AH1*, Issue 11

Was City Government in Late Nineteenth-Century America a "Conspicuous Failure"? *AH2*, Issue 6

Was Colonial American Culture Unique? *AH1*, Issue 1

Was Conflict Unavoidable Between Native Americans and Colonists? *AH1*, Issue 2

Was Dwight Eisenhower a Great President? *AH2*, Issue 13

Was John D. Rockefeller a "Robber Baron"? *AH2*, Issue 2

Was Martin Luther King, Jr's Leadership Essential to the Success of the Civil Rights Movement? *AH2*, Issue 15

Was Reconstruction a Total Failure? *AH1*, Issue 17, *AH2*, Issue 1

Was the American Labor Movement Radical? *AH2*, Issue 3

Was the Antebellum South a Unique Section in American History? *AH1*, Issue 15

Was the Colonial Period a "Golden Age" for Women in America? *AH1*, Issue 3

Was the Conflict Between the United States and Russia Inevitable? *AH2*, Issue 12

Was the Great Awakening a Key to the American Revolution? *AH1*, Issue 5

Was the New Deal an Effective Answer to the Great Depression? *AH2*, Issue 11

Was U.S. Foreign Policy in the Early Nineteenth Century Imperialistic? *AH1*, Issue 12

Was U.S. Intervention in Nicaragua in the Early Twentieth Century Motivated by "Dollar Diplomacy"? *AH2*, Issue 8

Were the Abolitionists "Unrestrained Fanatics"? *AH1*, Issue 14

Were the Immigrants' Old World Cultures Destroyed as They Adjusted to American Life? *AH2*, Issue 4

Were the Populists Democratic Reformers? *AH2*, Issue 5

Will AIDS Become a Middle-Class Heterosexual Disease? *HS*, Issue 10

Will Drug Legalization Help the Criminal Justice System? *CR*, Issue 17

Will Gun Control Reduce Crime? *CR*, Issue 15

Will the Canada-U.S. Free Trade Agreement Be Beneficial? *WP*, Issue 8

Will the Third World Pay Its Debt? *Eco*, Issue 17

Will Tougher Sentencing Reduce Crime? *Pol*, Issue 10

Topic Index

TOPIC INDEX

Sample Entry

①
Acid Rain

②
Is Immediate Action
Needed to Combat
the Effects of Acid
③
Rain? *Env*,
④
Issue 11

Explanatory Note

① topic

② issue in which
topic is covered

③ *Taking Sides*
volume in which
issue appears
(abbreviation)

④ issue number
within *Taking
Sides* volume

— A —

Abortion
Abortion: Should Public Officials
Protect the "Right to Choose"? *Pol*,
Issue 16
Is Abortion Always Immoral? *Mor*,
Issue 8
Is Abortion Immoral? *Bio*, Issue 1
Is the Antiabortion Movement Based on
a Belief in the Sacredness of Human
Life? *HS*, Issue 11
Should Prenatal Testing for Sex
Selection Be Permitted? *HS*, Issue 9
Should Research With Aborted Fetal
Tissue Be Banned? *Bio*, Issue 13
Should There Be a Right to Abortion?
Leg, Issue 9

Acid Rain
Is Immediate Action Needed to Combat
the Effects of Acid Rain? *Env*, Issue 11
Is the World Climate Threatened by
Global Warming? *WP*, Issue 19

Acquired Immune Deficiency
Syndrome. *See* AIDS

Affirmative action
Is Affirmative Action Constitutional?
Leg, Issue 11
Is Affirmative Action Morally Justified?
Mor, Issue 14
Is Affirmative Action Reverse
Discrimination? *Pol*, Issue 12, *Soc*,
Issue 9

Aggression
Does Behavioral Control Provide the
Best Learning Environment? *Edu*,
Issue 6
Is Rape Motivated by Aggression
Instead of Sex? *HS*, Issue 12

Aging
Does Welfare Do More Harm Than
Good? *Soc*, Issue 12
Should Health Care for the Elderly Be
Limited? *Bio*, Issue 19
Should the Police Do More to Manage
Street Life? *Leg*, Issue 4

Agriculture
Did President Jefferson Outfederalize
the Federalists? *AH1*, Issue 8
Is Population Control the Key to
Preventing Environmental
Deterioration? *Env*, Issue 6
Is the Environment Improving? *Soc*,
Issue 19
Is the Widespread Use of Pesticides
Required to Feed the World's People?
Env, Issue 9
Is the World Climate Threatened by
Global Warming? *WP*, Issue 19
Should We Try to Save the Family
Farm? *Eco*, Issue 2
Were the Populists Democrratic
Reformers? *AH2*, Issue 5

AIDS
Are Homosexual Relations Deviant? *Soc*,
Issue 14
Are There Limits to Confidentiality?
Bio, Issue 8
Does Government Have a Right to
Prohibit Homosexual Acts? *Pol*,
Issue 15
Should Insurance Companies Be
Allowed to Screen for Antibodies to
the AIDS Virus? *Bio*, Issue 18
Should the State Require All Family
Life Education Programs to Stress
Premarital Chastity and Monogamy?
HS, Issue 15
Should We Deregulate the Blood
Banking Industry? *Eco*, Issue 3
Will AIDS Become a Middle-Class
Heterosexual Disease? *HS*, Issue 10

Air pollution. *See* Pollution

Alcohol
Is Psychotherapy Effective? *Psy*, Issue 15

Will Drug Legalization Help the Criminal Justice System? *CR*, Issue 17

Alternative energy. *See also* **specific energies**
Is Nuclear Power Safe and Desirable? *Env*, Issue 8
Nuclear Waste: Was Yucca Mountain an Appropriate Site for Nuclear Waste Disposal? *Env*, Issue 15

American government. *See* **Bureaucracy; Congress; Judicial system; Presidency**

American history, Colonial
Can the Revolution Serve as a Developmental Model for Third World Nations Today? *AH1*, Issue 6
Did American Slaves Develop a Distinct Afro-American Culture in the Eighteenth Century? *AH1*, Issue 4
Was Colonial American Culture Unique? *AH1*, Issue 1
Was Conflict Unavoidable Between Native Americans and Colonists? *AH1*, Issue 2
Was the Colonial Period a "Golden Age" for Women in America? *AH1*, Issue 3
Was the Great Awakening a Key to the American Revolution? *AH1*, Issue 5

American history, Post–Civil War
Is Racial Oppression Declining in America? *Soc*, Issue 9
Was City Government in Late Nineteenth-Century America a "Conspicuous Failure"? *AH2*, Issue 6
Was John D. Rockefeller a "Robber Baron"? *AH2*, Issue 2
Was Reconstruction a Total Failure? *AH1*, Issue 17, *AH2*, Issue 1
Was the American Labor Movement Radical? *AH2*, Issue 3
Were the Immigrants' Old World Cultures Destroyed as They Adjusted to American Life? *AH2*, Issue 4
Were the Populists Democratic Reformers? *AH2*, Issue 5

American history, Pre–Civil War
Can the Revolution Serve as a Developmental Model for Third World Nations Today? *AH1*, Issue 6
Constitution, The: Was It an Economic Document? *AH1*, Issue 7

Did President Jefferson Outfederalize the Federalists? *AH1*, Issue 8
Did Slavery Destroy the Black Family? *AH1*, Issue 13
Did the Election of 1828 Represent a Democratic Revolt of the People? *AH1*, Issue 10
Did Women Achieve Greater Autonomy in the New Nation? *AH1*, Issue 9
Is American Intervention in Latin America Justified? *Pol*, Issue 18
Was Abraham Lincoln America's Greatest President? *AH1*, Issue 16
Was Antebellum Reform Motivated Primarily by Humanitarian Goals? *AH1*, Issue 11
Was the Antebellum South a Unique Section in American History? *AH1*, Issue 15
Was U.S. Foreign Policy in the Early Nineteenth Century Imperialistic? *AH1*, Issue 12
Were the Abolitionists "Unrestrained Fanatics"? *AH1*, Issue 14

American history, Twentieth Century
Could the United States Have Prevented the Fall of South Vietnam? *AH2*, Issue 14
Did the Progressives Fail? *AH2*, Issue 7
Did the Women's Movement Die in the 1920s? *AH2*, Issue 10
Did Woodrow Wilson Fail as Commander-in-Chief During World War I? *AH2*, Issue 9
Does an Elite Rule America? *Soc*, Issue 11
Has Congress Restricted Presidential War Powers Too Much? *Pol*, Issue 7
Is America Declining? *Pol*, Issue 20
Is America Headed for an Economic Bust? *Soc*, Issue 20
Is American Intervention in Latin America Justified? *Pol*, Issue 18
Is America Ruled by an Elite? *Pol*, Issue 1
Is the End of the Cold War in Sight? *Pol*, Issue 19
Is Racial Oppression Declining in America? *Soc*, Issue 9
Is the United States a Declining Power? *WP*, Issue 7
Was Dwight Eisenhower a Great President? *AH2*, Issue 13

Was Martin Luther King, Jr.'s
Leadership Essential to the Success of
the Civil Rights Movement? *AH2,*
Issue 15
Was the Conflict Between the United
States and Russia Inevitable? *AH2,*
Issue 12
Was the New Deal an Effective Answer
to the Great Depression? *AH2,*
Issue 11
Was U.S. Intervention in Nicaragua in
the Early Twentieth Century Motivated
by "Dollar Diplomacy"? *AH2,* Issue 8
Were the Immigrants' Old World
Cultures Destroyed as They Adjusted
to American Life? *AH2,* Issue 4

American Revolution
Can the Revolution Serve as a
Developmental Model for Third World
Nations Today? *AH1,* Issue 6
Was the Great Awakening a Key to the
American Revolution? *AH1,* Issue 5

American-Soviet relations. *See* **U.S.-
Soviet Union relations**

Animals. *See* **Wildlife**

Anxiety. *See* **Mental illness**

Armed forces. *See* **Military**

Arms limitation. *See* **SALT; START**

Arms race. *See* **Nuclear weapons**

Artificial insemination
Should Surrogate Motherhood Contracts
Be Illegal? *Leg,* Issue 12
Should Women Be Allowed to Bear
Babies for a Fee? *Bio,* Issue 3

Atomic bomb. *See* **Nuclear weapons**

Atomic energy. *See* **Nuclear energy**

Attorneys. *See* **Lawyers**

— B —

Banking
Should the Less Developed Countries
Pay Their International Debts? *WP,*
Issue 11
Will the Third World Pay Its Debt? *Eco,*
Issue 17

Behavior
Are Packaged Discipline Programs
Harmful? *Edu,* Issue 16

Does Behavioral Control Provide the
Best Learning Environment? *Edu,*
Issue 6
Is Our Behavior Primarily Determined
by Biological Processes? *Psy,* Issue 3
Is Involuntary Commitment Wrong?
Bio, Issue 9
Is The Sexual Revolution Over? *HS,*
Issue 1

Behavior disorders
Are Homosexual and Bisexual Relations
Natural and Normal? *HS,* Issue 3
Are Homosexual Relations Deviant? *Soc,*
Issue 14
Can Sex Be an Addiction? *HS,* Issue 6
Do Diagnostic Labels Hinder the
Effective Treatment of Persons With
Mental Disorders? *Psy,* Issue 13
Does Pornography Promote Sexual
Violence? *HS,* Issue 13
Is Criminal Behavior Biologically
Determined? *CR,* Issue 3
Is Involuntary Commitment Wrong?
Bio, Issue 9
Should the Insanity Defense Be
Abolished? *Leg,* Issue 17
Should the Use of the Principles of
Conditioning Be Limited in the
Modification of Undesirable Behavior?
Psy, Issue 7

Behavior modification
Did Women Achieve Greater Autonomy
in the New Nation? *AH1,* Issue 9
Does Behavioral Control Provide the
Best Learning Environment? *Edu,*
Issue 6
Is the Control of Human Behavior a
Proper Goal for Psychology? *Psy,*
Issue 19
Should Electroshock Therapy Be
Discontinued? *Psy,* Issue 15

Behavior therapy
Is Involuntary Commitment Wrong?
Bio, Issue 9
Should Electroshock Therapy Be
Discontinued? *Psy,* Issue 15

Bill of Rights. *See also* **American
Revolution; Constitution, U.S.**
Does Drug Use Testing Violate the
Fourth Amendment? *Leg,* Issue 6
Is Abortion Immoral? *Bio,* Issue 1
Should Handguns Be Banned? *Leg,*
Issue 16

Should Pornography Be Protected by the First Amendment? *Leg*, Issue 10

Should We Have a "Wall of Separation" Between Church and State? *Pol*, Issue 17

Will Gun Control Reduce Crime? *CR*, Issue 15

Biotechnology

Should Prenatal Testing for Sex Selection Be Permitted? *HS*, Issue 9

Should Research with Aborted Fetal Tissue Be Banned? *Bio*, Issue 13

Birth control

Are Abundant Resources and an Improved Environment Likely Future Prospects for the World's People? *Env*, Issue 19

Is Population Control the Key to Preventing Environmental Deterioration? *Env*, Issue 6

Birth defects

Should Parents Be Allowed to Decide to Withhold Treatment From Newborns with Birth Defects? *Bio*, Issue 7

Should Women Be Excluded from Jobs That Could Be Hazardous to a Fetus? *Env*, Issue 12

Blacks

Did American Slaves Develop a Distinct Afro-American Culture in the Eighteenth Century? *AH1*, Issue 4

Does Our Welfare System Hurt the Poor? *Pol*, Issue 14

Did Slavery Destroy the Black Family? *AH1*, Issue 13

Is Affirmative Action Constitutional? *Leg*, Issue 11

Is Affirmative Action Morally Justified? *Mor*, Issue 14

Is Affirmative Action Reverse Discrimination? *Pol*, Issue 12, *Soc*, Issue 10

Is the Criminal Justice System Racist? *CR*, Issue 8

Is Racial Oppression Declining in America? *Soc*, Issue 9

Is the Pain and Suffering Associated with Disinvestment and Sanctions Worth It for Black South African Workers? *Eco*, Issue 18

Should Strict Sanctions Be Applied Against South Africa? *WP*, Issue 4

Should Workers Be Paid According to "Comparable Worth"? *Pol*, Issue 13

Was Colonial American Culture Unique? *AH1*, Issue 1

Was Martin Luther King, Jr.'s Leadership Essential to the Success of the Civil Rights Movement? *AH2*, Issue 15

Was Reconstruction a Total Failure? *AH1*, Issue 17, *AH2*, Issue 1

Were the Abolitionists "Unrestrained Fanatics"? *AH1*, Issue 14

Brain chemistry

Is Criminal Behavior Biologically Determined? *CR*, Issue 3

Is Our Behavior Primarily Determined by Biological Processes? *Psy*, Issue 3

Brain Research

Has Science Discredited ESP? *Psy*, Issue 5

Is Our Behavior Primarily Determined by Biological Processes? *Psy*, Issue 3

Is the State of Hypnosis a Unique Altered State of Consciousness? *Psy*, Issue 6

Should Electroshock Therapy Be Discontinued? *Psy*, Issue 16

Bureaucracy

Does the Soviet Union Truly Want International Cooperation? *WP*, Issue 6

Has American Government Become Too Big? *Pol*, Issue 10

Was the New Deal an Effective Answer to the Great Depression? *AH2*, Issue 11

Business. *See* **Industry**

— C —

Campaigns, political

Do Political Action Committees Undermine Democracy? *Pol*, Issue 3

Have American Political Parties Lost Their Power? *Pol*, Issue 2

Should We Examine the Private Lives of Presidential Candidates? *Pol*, Issue 6

Cancer

Do Attitudes Affect Cancer? *Psy*, Issue 4

Does Risk-Benefit Analysis Provide an Objective Method for Making Environmental Decisions? *Env*, Issue 4

Is There a Cancer Epidemic Due to Industrial Chemicals in the Environment? *Env*, Issue 10

Is the Widespread Use of Pesticides Required to Feed the World's People? *Env*, Issue 9

Nuclear Waste: Was Yucca Mountain an Appropriate Site for Nuclear Waste Disposal? *Env*, Issue 15

Capital punishment. *See* **Death penalty**

Capitalism

Are Profits the Only Business of Business? *Eco*, Issue 1, *Mor*, Issue 15

Can Monetary and Fiscal Policies Still Be Used to Solve Our Macroeconomic Problems? *Eco*, Issue 11

Does Society Have an Obligation to Care for the Less Well Off? *Mor*, Issue 16

Is The Sexual Revolution Over? *HS*, Issue 1

Was John D. Rockefeller a "Robber Baron"? *AH2*, Issue 2

Was the American Labor Movement Radical? *AH2*, Issue 3

Was the Antebellum South a Unique Section in American History? *AH1*, Issue 15

Was the Conflict Between the United States and Russia Inevitable? *AH2*, Issue 12

Was the New Deal an Effective Answer to the Great Depression? *AH2*, Issue 11

Carcinogen. *See* **Cancer**

Checks and balances

Constitution, The: Was It an Economic Document? *AH1*, Issue 7

Does the Supreme Court Abuse Its Power? *Pol*, Issue 9

Has Congress Restricted Presidential War Powers Too Much? *Pol*, Issue 7

Should the U.S. Congress Limit the President's War Powers? *WP*, Issue 16

Should Congress Be Reformed? *Pol*, Issue 5

Chemicals, toxic. *See* **Toxic chemicals**

Child development

Are Traditional Families More Successful? *Soc*, Issue 5

Should Schooling Be Based on Students' Social Experiences? *Edu*, Issue 1

Should Very Young Children Receive Academic Instruction? *Edu*, Issue 12

Childrearing

Are Traditional Families More Successful? *Soc*, Issue 5

Can Women Combine Careers and Families? *Soc*, Issue 6

Did Slavery Destroy the Black Family? *AH1*, Issue 13

Does Welfare Do More Harm Than Good? *Soc*, Issue 13

Should Congress Guarantee U.S. Workers the Right to Parental Leave? *Eco*, Issue 8

Should Very Young Children Receive Academic Instruction? *Edu*, Issue 12

Church and state, Separation of

Is Church-State Separation Being Threatened? *Edu*, Issue 5

Should Prayer Be Permitted in Public Schools? *Leg*, Issue 8

Should We Have a "Wall of Separation" Between Church and State? *Pol*, Issue 17

Church, Roman Catholic

Abortion: Should Public Officials Protect The "Right to Choose"? *Pol*, Issue 16

Is the Antiabortion Movement Based on a Belief in the Sacredness of Human Life? *HS*, Issue 11

Civil rights. *See also* **Bill of Rights**

Does Drug Use Testing Violate the Fourth Amendment? *Leg*, Issue 6

Is "Comparable Worth" Worthless? *Eco*, Issue 4

Is It Unconstitutional to Discriminate Against Homosexuals? *Leg*, Issue 7

Is Racial Oppression Declining in America? *Soc*, Issue 9

Is the Victims' Rights Movement Succeeding? *CR*, Issue 18

Should Lawyers Use "Hardball" Tactics? *CR*, Issue 11

Should the Adversary System Be Abolished? *Leg*, Issue 1

Should the Police Do More to Manage Street Life? *Leg*, Issue 4

Should Workers Be Paid According to "Comparable Worth"? *Pol*, Issue 13

Was Abraham Lincoln America's
Greatest President? *AH1*, Issue 16
Was Martin Luther King, Jr.'s
Leadership Essential to the Success of
the Civil Rights Movement? *AH2*,
Issue 15

Civil War
Was Abraham Lincoln America's
Greatest President? *AH1*, Issue 16
Were the Abolitionists "Unrestrained
Fanatics"? *AH1*, Issue 14

Class discrimination
Constitution, The: Was It an Economic
Document? *AH1*, Issue 7
Did Women Achieve Greater Autonomy
in the New Nation? *AH1*, Issue 9

Climate
Does the Montreal Ozone Agreement
Signal a New Era of International
Environmental Statesmanship? *Env*,
Issue 18
Is Immediate Action Necessary to
Minimize Potential Catastrophic
Effects of Global Climatic Warming?
Env, Issue 17
Is the World Climate Threatened by
Global Warming? *WP*, Issue 19

Coal
Is Immediate Action Needed to Combat
the Effects of Acid Rain? *Env*, Issue 11
Is the World Climate Threatened by
Global Warming? *WP*, Issue 19

Cognitive development, child
Are Specific Programs to Teach
Thinking Needed? *Edu*, Issue 13
Are the Cards Stacked Against True
School Reform? *Edu*, Issue 9
Is Measurement-Driven Instruction
Desirable? *Edu*, Issue 15
Must All Students Be Given the Same
Kind of Schooling? *Edu*, Issue 10
Should Children Learn Morality
Primarily by Examining Their Own
Reasoning? *Psy*, Issue 9
Should Parents Provide Academic
Instruction for Their Children Before
They're Old Enough for School? *Psy*,
Issue 10
Should Values Be Developed Rather
Than Transmitted? *Edu*, Issue 4
Should Very Young Children Receive
Academic Instruction? *Edu*, Issue 12

Cognitive processes
Are Specific Programs To Teach
Thinking Needed? *Edu*, Issue 13
Can Computers Think? *Psy*, Issue 8
Should Children Learn Morality
Primarily by Examining Their Own
Reasoning? *Psy*, Issue 9
Should Parents Provide Academic
Instruction for Their Children Before
They're Old Enough for School? *Psy*,
Issue 10
Should Values Be Developed Rather
Than Transmitted? *Edu*, Issue 4
Should Very Young Children Receive
Academic Instruction? *Edu*, Issue 12

Colonialism
Did American Slaves Develop a Distinct
Afro-American Culture in the
Eighteenth Century? *AH1*, Issue 4
Is the Third World Responsible for Its
Own Lack of Economic Development?
WP, Issue 10
Was Colonial American Culture Unique?
AH1, Issue 1
Was Conflict Unavoidable Between
Native Americans and Colonists? *AH1*,
Issue 2
Was the Colonial Period a "Golden
Age" for Women in America? *AH1*,
Issue 3
Was the Great Awakening a Key to the
American Revolution? *AH1*, Issue 5

Communism
Does the Soviet Union Truly Want
International Cooperation? *WP*, Issue 6
Is the End of the Cold War in Sight?
Pol, Issue 19
Is the United States Becoming Too
Friendly with China? *WP*, Issue 1
Is U.S. Intervention in Latin America
and Elsewhere Justified? *WP*, Issue 3
Should Morality and Human Rights
Strongly Influence Foreign
Policymaking? *WP*, Issue 15
Was the Conflict Between the United
States and Russia Inevitable? *AH2*,
Issue 12

Computers
Can Computers Think? *Psy*, Issue 8
Should Parents Provide Academic
Instruction for Their Children Before
They're Old Enough for Schools? *Psy*,
Issue 10

Congress

Are Official Statistics Meaningful? *CR*, Issue 5

Are There Too Many Hostile Takeovers? *Eco*, Issue 5

Has Congress Restricted Presidential War Powers Too Much? *Pol*, Issue 7

Is Tax Reform an Impossible Dream Come True? *Eco*, Issue 12

Nuclear Waste: Was Yucca Mountain an Appropriate Site for Nuclear Waste Disposal? *Env*, Issue 15

Should Congress Be Reformed? *Pol*, Issue 5

Should Congress Guarantee U.S. Workers the Right to Parental Leave? *Eco*, Issue 8

Should the U.S. Congress Limit the President's War Powers? *WP*, Issue 16

Conservation

Are Abundant Resources and an Improved Environment Likely Future Prospects for the World's People? *Env*, Issue 19

Does Wilderness Have Intrinsic Value? *Env*, Issue 1

Do We Need More Stringently Enforced Regulations to Protect Endangered Species? *Env*, Issue 2

Is EPA's Strategy Evolving to Meet Present and Future Environmental Problems? *Env.*, Issue 13

Conservatism

Do the News Media Have a Liberal Bias? *Pol*, Issue 4

Has American Government Become Too Big? *Eco*, Issue 10

Constitution, U.S. *See also* Bill of Rights

Constitution, The: Was It an Economic Document? *AH1*, Issue 7

Did the Women's Movement Die in the 1920s? *AH2*, Issue 10

Does an Elite Rule America? *Soc*, Issue 11

Does Drug Use Testing Violate the Fourth Amendment? *Leg*, Issue 6

Does Government Have a Constitutional Right to Prohibit Certain Kinds of Sexual Conduct? *HS*, Issue 14

Does Government Have a Right to Prohibit Homosexual Acts? *Pol*, Issue 15

Does the Supreme Court Abuse Its Power? *Pol*, Issue 9

Is Affirmative Action Constitutional? *Leg*, Issue 11

Is Capital Punishment Justified? *Pol*, Issue 11

Is Church-State Separation Being Threatened? *Edu*, Issue 5

Is It Unconstitutional to Discriminate Against Homosexuals? *Leg*, Issue 7

Should Prayer Be Permitted in Public Schools? *Leg*, Issue 8

Should There Be a Right to Abortion? *Leg*, Issue 9

Should the U.S. Congress Limit the President's War Powers? *WP*, Issue 16

Should We Have a "Wall of Separation" Between Church and State? *Pol*, Issue 17

Consumer health. *See* Health care

Consumerism

Are Profits the Only Business of Business? *Eco*, Issue 1, *Mor*, Issue 15

Does the Government Regulate Too Much? *Pol*, Issue 8

Has Individualism Become Excessive? *Soc*, Issue 3

Is America Headed for an Economic Bust? *Soc*, Issue 20

Is the Environment Improving? *Soc*, Issue 19

Is The Sexual Revolution Over? *HS*, Issue 1

Contraception. *See* Birth control

Corporations, U.S. *See* Industry

Corrections system

Is Incapacitation the Answer to the Crime Problem? *Soc*, Issue 15

Should Capital Punishment Be Abolished? *CR*, Issue 13, *Mor*, Issue 11

Should the Death Penalty Be Abolished? *Leg*, Issue 14

Will Tougher Sentencing Reduce Crime? *Pol*, Issue 10

Counseling. *See* Psychotherapy

Court system. *See* Judicial system; Supreme Court

Crime. *See also* **Corrections system; Crime prevention; Criminal behavior; Criminal justice system; Death penalty**

Are Official Statistics Meaningful? *CR*, Issue 5

Do We Have a Moral Responsibility to Rehabilitate Criminals? *Mor*, Issue 10

Do We Need More Jails? *CR*, Issue 14

Has the Women's Movement Increased Female Criminality? *CR*, Issue 7

Is Capital Punishment Justified? *Pol*, Issue 11

Is Crime Created by Society's Elites? *CR*, Issue 2

Is Crime Functional? *CR*, Issue 1

Is Crime Getting Worse? *CR*, Issue 6

Is Criminal Behavior Biologically Determined? *CR*, Issue 3

Is Incapacitation the Answer to the Crime Problem? *Soc*, Issue 15

Is "Killing" the Same as "Letting Die"? *Bio*, Issue 5

Is Pornography Harmful? *Psy*, Issue 17

Is Rape Motivated by Aggression Instead of Sex? *HS*, Issue 12

Is Street Crime More Serious Than White-Collar Crime? *CR*, Issue 4

Is the Criminal Justice System Racist? *CR*, Issue 8

Is the Victims' Rights Movement Succeeding? *CR*, Issue 18

Is Urban Life Crazy? *Soc*, Issue 4

Juvenile Justice: Are Kids "Getting Away With Murder"? *CR*, Issue 10

Should Handguns Be Banned? *Leg*, Issue 16

Should Immigration Be More Limited? *Soc*, Issue 16

Should Insanity Be Considered a Legal Defense for Criminals? *Psy*, Issue 18

Should Prostitution Be Decriminalized? *HS*, Issue 17

Should the Law Enforce Morality? *Mor*, Issue 13

Should the Police Direct Community Crime Prevention? *CR*, Issue 9

Should the Police Do More to Manage Street Life? *Leg*, Issue 4

Will Gun Control Reduce Crime? *CR*, Issue 15

Will Tougher Sentencing Reduce Crime? *Pol*, Issue 10

Crime prevention. *See also* **Crime**

Is Incapacitation the Answer to the Crime Problem? *Soc*, Issue 15

Juvenile Justice: Are Kids "Getting Away With Murder"? *CR*, Issue 10

Should Immigration Be More Limited? *Soc*, Issue 16

Is Selective Incapacitation Just? *CR*, Issue 12

Should the Police Direct Community Crime Prevention? *CR*, Issue 9

Should the Police Do More to Manage Street Life? *Leg*, Issue 4

Will Tougher Sentencing Reduce Crime? *Pol*, Issue 10

Criminal behavior. *See also* **Crime**

Are Official Statistics Meaningful? *CR*, Issue 5

Do the Ends Justify the Means? *Mor*, Issue 5

Do We Have a Moral Responsibility to Rehabilitate Criminals? *Mor*, Issue 10

Has the Women's Movement Increased Female Criminality? *CR*, Issue 7

Is Crime Created by Society's Elites? *CR*, Issue 2

Is Crime Functional? *CR*, Issue 1

Is Criminal Behavior Biologically Determined? *CR*, Issue 3

Is Incapacitation the Answer to the Crime Problem? *Soc*, Issue 15

Is Rape Motivated by Aggression Instead of Sex? *HS*, Issue 12

Is Selective Incapacitation Just? *CR*, Issue 12

Is Street Crime More Serious Than White-Collar Crime? *CR*, Issue 4

Should Insanity Be Considered a Legal Defense for Criminals? *Psy*, Issue 18

Should Prostitution Be Decriminalized? *HS*, Issue 17

Should the Insanity Defense Be Abolished? *Leg*, Issue 17

Should the Police Do More to Manage Street Life? *Leg*, Issue 4

Criminal justice system. *See also* **Crime**

Are Official Statistics Meaningful? *CR*, Issue 5

Do We Have a Moral Responsibility to Rehabilitate Criminals? *Mor*, Issue 10

Do We Need More Jails? *CR*, Issue 14

Has the Women's Movement Increased Female Criminality? *CR*, Issue 7
Is Crime Functional? *CR*, Issue 1
Is Crime Getting Worse? *CR*, Issue 6
Is Euthanasia Immoral? *Soc*, Issue 7
Is Incapacitation the Answer to the Crime Problem? *Soc*, Issue 15
Is Selective Incapacitation Just? *CR*, Issue 12
Is the Criminal Justice System Racist? *CR*, Issue 8
Is the Victims' Rights Movement Succeeding? *CR*, Issue 18
Juvenile Justice: Are Kids "Getting Away With Murder"? *CR*, Issue 10
Should Capital Punishment Be Abolished? *CR*, Issue 13, *Mor*, Issue 11
Should Immigration Be More Limited? *Soc*, Issue 16
Should Insanity Be Considered a Legal Defense for Criminals? *Psy*, Issue 18
Should Lawyers Use "Hardball" Tactics? *CR*, Issue 11
Should Plea Bargaining Be Abolished? *Leg*, Issue 3
Should the Death Penalty Be Abolished? *Leg*, Issue 14
Should the Exclusionary Rule Be Abolished? *Leg*, Issue 15
Should We Send Convicts to Penal Colonies? *CR*, Issue 16
Will Drug Legalization Help the Criminal Justice System? *CR*, Issue 17
Will Tougher Sentencing Reduce Crime? *Pol*, Issue 10

Criminals. *See* **Crime; Criminal behavior**

Culture, American

Are Packaged Discipline Programs Harmful? *Edu*, Issue 16
Are Traditional Families More Successful? *Soc*, Issue 5
Can Suicide Be Rational? *Psy*, Issue 14
Did American Slaves Develop a Distinct Afro-American Culture in the Eighteenth Century? *AH1*, Issue 4
Did the Progressives Fail? *AH2*, Issue 7
Does "Lower-Class" Culture Perpetuate Poverty? *Soc*, Issue 2
Does Wilderness Have Intrinsic Value? *Env*, Issue 1
Do the Ends Justify the Means? *Mor*, Issue 5
Do We Have a Moral Right to Die? *Mor*, Issue 6
Has Individualism Become Excessive? *Soc*, Issue 3
Is Bilingual Education Justifiable as a Policy? *Edu*, Issue 19
Is Incapacitation the Answer to the Crime Problem? *Soc*, Issue 15
Is Monogamy the Best Form of Marriage? *HS*, Issue 5
Is Morality Relative? *Mor*, Issue 1
Is The "New Woman" the Main Cause of Turmoil and Tension in Male/Female Relations Today? *HS*, Issue 2
Is The Sexual Revolution Over? *HS*, Issue 1
Should Curricula Emphasize Commonality Over Diversity? *Edu*, Issue 3
Should Literacy Be Based on Traditional Culture? *Edu*, Issue 14
Was Colonial American Culture Unique? *AH1*, Issue 1
Were the Immigrants' Old World Cultures Destroyed as They Adjusted to American Life? *AH2*, Issue 4
Were the Populists Democratic Reformers? *AH2*, Issue 5

— D —

Death and dying. *See also* **Euthanasia; Suicide**

Can Suicide Be Rational? *Psy*, Issue 14
Do Patients Have a Right to Die? *Leg*, Issue 13
Do We Have a Moral Right to Die? *Mor*, Issue 6
Is Euthanasia Immoral? *Mor*, Issue 7
Is It Ethical to Implant Animal Hearts in Humans? *Bio*, Issue 12
Is It Ethical to Withhold the Truth From Dying Patients? *Bio*, Issue 4
Is "Killing" the Same as "Letting Die"? *Bio*, Issue 5
Must Fluids and Nutrition Always Be Given To Dying Patients? *Bio*, Issue 6
Nuclear Waste: Was Yucca Mountain an Appropriate Site for Nuclear Waste Disposal? *Env*, Issue 15
Should Newborns Without Brains Be Used As Organ Donors? *Bio*, Issue 16

Should Organ Procurement Be Based on Voluntarism? *Bio*, Issue 15

Death penalty
Is Capital Punishment Justified? *Pol*, Issue 11
Is the Criminal Justice System Racist? *CR*, Issue 8
Should Capital Punishment Be Abolished? *CR*, Issue 13, *Mor*, Issue 11
Should the Death Penalty Be Abolished? *Leg*, Issue 14

Declaration of Independence
Is Affirmative Action Constitutional? *Leg*, Issue 11
Is America Ruled by an Elite? *Pol*, Issue 1
Was Abraham Lincoln America's Greatest President? *AH1*, Issue 16

Deforestation. *See* **Forests**

Democracy
Do Political Action Committees Undermine Democracy? *Pol*, Issue 3
Should the U.S. Congress Limit the President's War Powers? *WP*, Issue 16
Was the Conflict Between the United States and Russia Inevitable? *AH2*, Issue 12
Was the Great Awakening a Key to the American Revolution? *AH1*, Issue 5
Were the Populists Democratic Reformers? *AH2*, Issue 5

Democratic party
Did the Election of 1828 Represent a Democratic Revolt of the People? *AH1*, Issue 10
Have American Political Parties Lost Their Power? *Pol*, Issue 2

Deregulation. *See* **Government regulation**

Desegregation. *See* **Racial discrimination**

Deviant behavior. *See* **Behavior disorders**

Disabled people. *See* **Handicapism**

Discrimination. *See* **Class discrimination; Ethnic discrimination; Handicapism; Racial discrimination; Sex discrimination**

Disease. *See also* **specific diseases**
Are Homosexual Relations Deviant? *Soc*, Issue 14

Are There Limits to Confidentiality? *Bio*, Issue 8
Do Attitudes Affect Cancer? *Psy*, Issue 4
Is It Ethical to Withhold the Truth From Dying Patients? *Bio*, Issue 4
Should Insurance Companies Be Allowed to Screen for Antibodies to the AIDS Virus? *Bio*, Issue 18
Should Newborns Without Brains Be Used As Organ Donors? *Bio*, Issue 16
Should Research With Aborted Fetal Tissue Be Banned? *Bio*, Issue 13
Should We Deregulate the Blood Banking Industry? *Eco*, Issue 3
Will AIDS Become a Middle-Class Heterosexual Disease? *HS*, Issue 10

Divorce
Is Monogamy the Best Form of Marriage? *HS*, Issue 5
Is The Welfare System Causing Poverty? *Eco*, Issue 13

DNA. *See* **Genetics**

Drug abuse
Does Drug Use Testing Violate the Fourth Amendment? *Leg*, Issue 6
Will AIDS Become a Middle-Class Heterosexual Disease? *HS*, Issue 10
Will Drug Legalization Help the Criminal Justice System? *CR*, Issue 17

Dumping
Municipal Waste: Is Modern Waste Incineration Technology an Environmentally Benign Alternative to Garbage Dumps? *Env*, Issue 14
Nuclear Waste: Was Yucca Mountain an Appropriate Site for Nuclear Waste Disposal? *Env.*, Issue 15

Dying. *See* **Death and dying**

— E —

Economic growth
Are Abundant Resources and an Improved Environment Likely Future Prospects for the World's People? *Env*, Issue 19
Can Monetary and Fiscal Policies Still Be Used to Solve Our Macroeconomic Problems? *Eco*, Issue 11

Does Society Have an Obligation to Care for the Less Well Off? *Mor*, Issue 16

Do Firms Exploit Workers and Local Communities By Closing Profitable Plants? *Eco*, Issue 7

Do Foreign Investments Threaten U.S. Economic Independence? *WP*, Issue 9

Has American Government Become Too Big? *Eco*, Issue 10

Has American Government Gotten Too Big? *Soc*, Issue 12

Is America Declining? *Pol*, Issue 20

Is America Headed for an Economic Bust? *Soc*, Issue 20

Is Crime Getting Worse? *CR*, Issue 6

Is Manufacturing Alive and Well and Living in the U.S.? *Eco*, Issue 20

Is the Third World Responsible for Its Own Lack of Economic Development? *WP*, Issue 10

Is the United States a Declining Power? *WP*, Issue 7

Should Schools Serve National Economic Needs? *Edu*, Issue 8

Should the Less Developed Countries Pay Their International Debts? *WP*, Issue 11

Should We Try To Save the Family Farm? *Eco*, Issue 2

Was City Government in Late Nineteenth-Century America a "Conspicuous Failure"? *AH2*, Issue 6

Was John D. Rockefeller a "Robber Baron"? *AH2*, Issue 2

Was the Colonial Period a "Golden Age" for Women in America? *AH1*, Issue 3

Will the Canada-U.S. Free Trade Agreement Be Beneficial? *WP*, Issue 8

Economic history, Colonial
Can the Revolution Serve as a Developmental Model for Third World Nations Today? *AH1*, Issue 6

Was the Colonial Period a "Golden Age" for Women in America? *AH1*, Issue 3

Economic history, Post–Civil War
Are There Too Many Hostile Takeovers? *Eco*, Issue 5

Was Reconstruction a Total Failure? *AH1*, Issue 17, *AH2*, Issue 1

Was the American Labor Movement Radical? *AH2*, Issue 3

Was U.S. Intervention in Nicaragua in the Early Twentieth Century Motivated by "Dollar Diplomacy"? *AH2*, Issue 8

Economic history, Pre–Civil War
Constitution, The: Was It an Economic Document? *AH1*, Issue 7

Did President Jefferson Outfederalize the Federalists? *AH1*, Issue 8

Was the Antebellum South a Unique Section in American History? *AH1*, Issue 15

Economic history, Twentieth Century
Are There Too Many Hostile Takeovers? *Eco*, Issue 5

Can Monetary and Fiscal Policies Still Be Used to Solve Our Macroeconomic Problems? *Eco*, Issue 11

Did Monetary Policy Cause the Stock Market Crash of 1987? *Eco*, Issue 15

Do Foreign Investments Threaten U.S. Economic Independence? *WP*, Issue 9

Is the United States in a Period of Decline? *AH2*, Issue 16

Should We Try to Save the Family Farm? *Eco*, Issue 2

Was the Conflict Between the United States and Russia Inevitable? *AH2*, Issue 12

Was the New Deal an Effective Answer to the Great Depression? *AH2*, Issue 11

Was U.S. Intervention in Nicaragua in the Early Twentieth Century Motivated by "Dollar Diplomacy"? *AH2*, Issue 8

Economic philosophy
Are Profits the Only Business of Business? *Eco*, Issue 1, *Mor*, Issue 15

Can Monetary and Fiscal Policies Still Be Used to Solve Our Macroeconomic Problems? *Eco*, Issue 11

Should The Federal Government Deregulate American Business? *Eco*, Issue 6

Education. *See* **Cognitive development, child; Intelligence; Learning; Schools**

Elections
Did the Election of 1828 Represent a Democratic Revolt of the People? *AH1*, Issue 10

Should We Examine the Private Lives of President Candidates? *Pol*, Issue 6

Employment
Did Women Achieve Greater Autonomy in the New Nation? *AH1*, Issue 9
Does Drug Use Testing Violate the Fourth Amendment? *Leg*, Issue 6
Does "Lower Class" Culture Perpetuate Poverty? *Soc*, Issue 2
Is It Time to Abolish the Minimum Wage? *Eco*, Issue 9
Is Manufacturing Alive and Well and Living in the U.S.? *Eco*, Issue 20
Should Immigration Be More Limited? *Soc*, Issue 16

Endangered species. *See* **Wildlife**

Energy issues. *See also* **specific fuels and energies**
Is Nuclear Power Safe and Desirable? *Env*, Issue 8
Nuclear Waste: Was Yucca Mountain an Appropriate Site for Nuclear Waste Disposal? *Env*, Issue 15
Should Regulation of Airborne Toxins Under the Clean Air Act Be Strengthened? *Env*, Issue 7

Environment. *See also* **Environmental laws**
Are Abundant Resources and an Improved Environment Likely Future Prospects for the World's People? *Env*, Issue 19
Are Environmentalists and Industrial Leaders Becoming Less Adversarial? *Env*, Issue 5
Does Risk-Benefit Analysis Provide an Objective Method for Making Environmental Decisions? *Env*, Issue 4
Does the Montreal Ozone Agreement Signal a New Era of International Environmental Statesmanship? *Env*, Issue 18
Does Wilderness Have Intrinsic Value? *Env*, Issue 1
Do We Need More Stringently Enforced Regulations to Protect Endangered Species? *Env*, Issue 2
Is EPA's Strategy Evolving to Meet Present and Future Environmental Problems? *Env*, Issue 3
Is Immediate Action Necessary to Minimize Potential Catastrophic Effects of Global Climatic Warming? *Env*, Issue 17

Is Immediate Action Needed to Combat the Effects of Acid Rain? *Env*, Issue 11
Is Nuclear Power Safe and Desirable? *Env*, Issue 8
Is Population Control the Key to Preventing Environmental Deterioration? *Env*, Issue 6
Is the Environment Improving? *Soc*, Issue 19
Is There a Cancer Epidemic Due to Industrial Chemicals in the Environment? *Env*, Issue 10
Is the United Nations a Beneficial Organization? *WP*, Issue 18
Is the Widespread Use of Pesticides Required to Feed the World's People? *Env*, Issue 9
Is the World Climate Threatened by Global Warming? *WP*, Issue 19
Is the World Threatened by a Population Bomb? *Soc*, Issue 18
Municipal Waste: Is Modern Incineration Technology an Environmentally Benign Alternative to Garbage Dumps? *Env*, Issue 14

Environmental laws
Does Risk-Benefit Analysis Provide an Objective Method for Making Environmental Decisions? *Env*, Issue 4
Does the Montreal Ozone Agreement Signal a New Era of International Environmental Statesmanship? *Env*, Issue 18
Does Wilderness Have Intrinsic Value? *Env*, Issue 1
Do We Need More Stringently Enforced Regulations to Protect Endangered Species? *Env*, Issue 2
Is the Environment Improving? *Soc*, Issue 19
Should Regulation of Airborne Toxins Under the Clean Air Act Be Strengthened? *Env*, Issue 7
Was Dwight Eisenhower a Great President? *AH2*, Issue 13

Equality *See* **Blacks; Ethnic discrimination; Minorities; Racial discrimination; Sex discrimination; Women's issues**

ERA. *See* **Bill of Rights; Sex discrimination**

Ethical issues

Abortion: Should Public Officials Protect The "Right to Choose"? *Pol*, Issue 16

Are Homosexual Relations Deviant? *Soc*, Issue 14

Are There Limits to Confidentiality? *Bio*, Issue 8

Can Deception in Psychological Research Be Justified? *Psy*, Issue 1

Can Deception in Research Be Justified? *Bio*, Issue 11

Does Morality Require Nuclear Disarmament? *Mor*, Issue 18

Do Rich Nations Have an Obligation to Help Poor Nations? *Mor*, Issue 17

Do Surrogate Motherhood Contracts Exploit Women? *HS*, Issue 18

Do the Ends Justify the Means? *Mor*, Issue 5

Do We Have a Moral Responsibility to Rehabilitate Criminals? *Mor*, Issue 10

Do We Have a Moral Right to Die? *Mor*, Issue 6

Has Individualism Become Excessive? *Soc*, Issue 3

Is Abortion Always Immoral? *Mor*, Issue 8

Is Abortion Immoral? *Bio*, Issue 1

Is Affirmative Action Morally Justified? *Mor*, Issue 14

Is Crime Functional? *CR*, Issue 1

Is Euthanasia Immoral? *Mor*, Issue 7

Is Extramarital Sex Wrong? *Mor*, Issue 9

Is Genetic Engineering a Threat to Future Generations? *Bio*, Issue 20

Is It Ethical to Implant Animal Hearts in Humans? *Bio*, Issue 12

Is It Wrong To Create Test-Tube Babies? *Bio*, Issue 2

Is It Wrong to "Politicize" Sociology? *Soc*, Issue 1

Is "Killing" the Same as "Letting Die"? *Bio*, Issue 5

Is Morality Subjective? *Mor*, Issue 2

Is Morality the Exclusive Province of Religion? *Mor*, Issue 3

Is Pornography a Threat to Society? *Mor*, Issue 12

Is the Control of Human Behavior a Proper Goal for Psychology? *Psy*, Issue 19

Is the Legal Profession Declining? *Leg*, Issue 5

Must Fluids and Nutrition Always Be Given To Dying Patients? *Bio*, Issue 6

Should Animal Experimentation Be Permitted? *Bio*, Issue 14

Should Doctors Cut Costs at the Bedside? *Bio*, Issue 10

Should Health Care for the Elderly Be Limited? *Bio*, Issue 19

Should Insanity Be Considered a Legal Defense for Criminals? *Psy*, Issue 18

Should Insurance Companies Be Allowed to Screen for Antibodies to the AIDS Virus? *Bio*, Issue 18

Should Morality and Human Rights Strongly Influence Foreign Policymaking? *WP*, Issue 15

Should Newborns Without Brains Be Used as Organ Donors? *Bio*, Issue 16

Should Organ Procurement Be Based on Voluntarism? *Bio*, Issue 15

Should Parents Be Allowed to Decide to Withhold Treatment From Newborns with Birth Defects? *Bio*, Issue 7

Should Prenatal Testing for Sex Selection Be Permitted? *HS*, Issue 9

Should Prostitution Be Decriminalized? *HS*, Issue 17

Should Research With Aborted Fetal Tissue Be Banned? *Bio*, Issue 13

Should the Adversary System Be Abolished? *Leg*, Issue 1

Should the Insanity Defense Be Abolished? *Leg*, Issue 17

Should There Be a Market in Body Parts? *Bio*, Issue 17

Should the State Require All Family Life Education Programs to Stress Premarital Chastity and Monogamy? *HS*, Issue 15

Should Values Be Developed Rather Than Transmitted? *Edu*, Issue 4

Was Dwight Eisenhower a Great President? *AH2*, Issue 13

Ethnic discrimination

Is Bilingual Education Justifiable as a Policy? *Edu*, Issue 19

Should the Law Enforce Morality? *Mor*, Issue 13

Should the Use of the Principles of Conditioning Be Limited in the Modification of Undesirable Behavior? *Psy*, Issue 7

Were the Populists Democratic Reformers? *AH2*, Issue 5

Euthanasia
Is Euthanasia Immoral? *Mor*, Issue 7
Is "Killing" the Same as "Letting Die"? *Bio*, Issue 5
Must Fluids and Nutrition Always Be Given To Dying Patients? *Bio*, Issue 6
Should Parents Be Allowed to Decide to Withhold Treatment From Newborns with Birth Defects? *Bio*, Issue 7

— F —

Family structure
Are Packaged Discipline Programs Harmful? *Edu*, Issue 16
Are Traditional Families More Successful? *Soc*, Issue 5
Did American Slaves Develop a Distinct Afro-American Culture in the Eighteenth Century? *AH1*, Issue 4
Did Slavery Destroy the Black Family? *AH1*, Issue 13
Does Our Welfare System Hurt the Poor? *Pol*, Issue 14
Is Sex Education in Schools an Attempt to Institutionalize a Sexual Revolution? *HS*, Issue 7
Is The Sexual Revolution Over? *HS*, Issue 1
Should Congress Guarantee U.S. Workers the Right to Parental Leave? *Eco*, Issue 8
Should Surrogate Motherhood Contracts Be Illegal? *Leg*, Issue 12
Should the State Require All Family Life Education Programs to Stress Premarital Chastity and Monogamy? *HS*, Issue 15
Should Women Be Allowed to Bear Babies for a Fee? *Bio*, Issue 3
Were the Immigrants' Old World Cultures Destroyed as They Adjusted to American Life? *AH2*, Issue 4

Farming. *See* **Agriculture**

Fathering. *See also* **Mothering; Parenting**
Did Slavery Destroy the Black Family? *AH1*, Issue 13
Should There Be a Right to Abortion? *Leg*, Issue 9

Federal budget
Can Federal Budget Deficits Be Good for the Economy? *Eco*, Issue 14
Is America Headed for an Economic Bust? *Soc*, Issue 20

Federal government. *See also* **Bureaucracy**
Are Proposed Elementary School Reforms Realistic? *Edu*, Issue 11
Can Federal Budget Deficits Be Good for the Economy? *Eco*, Issue 14
Constitution, The: Was It an Economic Document? *AH1*, Issue 7
Does an Elite Rule America? *Soc*, Issue 11
Does Drug Use Testing Violate the Fourth Amendment? *Leg*, Issue 6
Does Government Have a Constitutional Right to Prohibit Certain Kinds of Sexual Conduct? *HS*, Issue 14
Does Government Have a Right to Prohibit Homosexual Acts? *Pol*, Issue 15
Does the Government Regulate Too Much? *Pol*, Issue 8
Do We Need More Stringently Enforced Regulations to Protect Endangered Species? *Env*, Issue 2
Do We Need New Federal Legislation to Protect the Future Integrity of Our Groundwater? *Env*, Issue 16
Has American Government Become Too Big? *Eco*, Issue 10
Has American Government Gotten Too Big? *Soc*, Issue 12
Has Congress Restricted Presidential War Powers Too Much? *Pol*, Issue 7
Is America Ruled by an Elite? *Pol*, Issue 1
Is EPA's Strategy Evolving to Meet Present and Future Environmental Problems? *Env*, Issue 3
Is Mainstreaming Beneficial to All? *Edu*, Issue 17
Is Pornography Harmful? *Psy*, Issue 17
Is Tax Reform an Impossible Dream Come True? *Eco*, Issue 12
Should Doctors Cut Costs at the Bedside? *Bio*, Issue 10
Should Handguns Be Banned? *Leg*, Issue 16

Should the Federal Government
Deregulate American Business? *Eco*,
Issue 6

Should We Have a "Wall of Separation"
Between Church and State? *Pol*,
Issue 17

Was Reconstruction a Total Failure?
AH1, Issue 17, *AH2*, Issue 1

Federal Reserve System

Are There Too Many Hostile Takeovers?
Eco, Issue 5

Can Federal Budget Deficits Be Good
for the Economy? *Eco*, Issue 14

Can Monetary and Fiscal Policies Still
Be Used to Solve Our Macroeconomic
Problems? *Eco*, Issue 11

Should We Try to Save the Family
Farm? *Eco*, Issue 2

Feminism. *See* **Women's issues**

Food supply

Is the Third World Responsible for Its
Own Lack of Economic Development?
WP, Issue 10

Is the Widespread Use of Pesticides
Required to Feed the World's People?
Env, Issue 9

Is the World Threatened by a
Population Bomb? *Soc*, Issue 18

Foreign policy, American

Could the United States Have
Prevented the Fall of South Vietnam?
AH2, Issue 14

Did Woodrow Wilson Fail as
Commander-in-Chief During World
War I? *AH2*, Issue 9

Should Morality and Human Rights
Strongly Influence Foreign
Policymaking? *WP*, Issue 15

Was Dwight Eisenhower a Great
President? *AH2*, Issue 13

Was U.S. Foreign Policy in the Early
Nineteenth Century Imperialistic?
AH1, Issue 12

Was U.S. Intervention in Nicaragua in
the Early Twentieth Century Motivated
by "Dollar Diplomacy"? *AH2*, Issue 8

Will the Third World Pay Its Debt? *Eco*,
Issue 17

Forests

Does Wilderness Have Intrinsic Value?
Env, Issue 1

Is Immediate Action Necessary to
Minimize Potential Catastrophic

Effects of Global Climatic Warming?
Env, Issue 17

Is Immediate Action Needed to Combat
the Effects of Acid Rain? *Env*, Issue 11

Is the World Climate Threatened by
Global Warming? *WP*, Issue 19

Fossil fuels

Is Immediate Action Needed to Combat
the Effects of Acid Rain? *Env*, Issue 11

Is the World Climate Threatened by
Global Warming? *WP*, Issue 19

Fuel. *See* **specific sources of fuel**

Future

Are Abundant Resources and an
Improved Environment Likely Future
Prospects for the World's People? *Env*,
Issue 19

Are Proposed Elementary School
Reforms Realistic? *Edu*, Issue 11

Could NATO Forces Withstand a
Conventional Attack by the Warsaw
Pact? *WP*, Issue 12

Do We Need New Federal Legislation to
Protect the Future Integrity of Our
Groundwater? *Env*, Issue 16

Is EPA's Strategy Evolving to Meet
Present and Future Environmental
Problems? *Env*, Issue 3

Is Genetic Engineering a Threat to
Future Generations? *Bio*, Issue 20

Is Immediate Action Necessary to
Minimize Potential Catastrophic
Effects of Global Climatic Warming?
Env, Issue 17

Is the Middle Class Shrinking? *Eco*,
Issue 19

Is the World Threatened by a
Population Bomb? *Soc*, Issue 18

Should Immigration Be More Limited?
Soc, Issue 16

Will the Canada-U.S. Free Trade
Agreement Be Beneficial? *WP*, Issue 8

— G —

Genetics

Is Criminal Behavior Biologically
Determined? *CR*, Issue 3

Is Genetic Engineering a Threat to
Future Generations? *Bio*, Issue 20

Should Prenatal Testing for Sex
Selection Be Permitted? *HS*, Issue 9

GNP
Does Welfare Do More Harm Than
Good? *Soc*, Issue 13
Has American Government Gotten Too
Big? *Soc*, Issue 12

Government regulation
Are Environmentalists and Industrial
Leaders Becoming Less Adversarial?
Env, Issue 5
Does the Government Regulate Too
Much? *Pol*, Issue 8
Does Welfare Do More Harm Than
Good? *Soc*, Issue 13
Do We Need New Federal Legislation to
Protect the Future Integrity of Our
Groundwater? *Env*, Issue 16
Has American Government Become Too
Big? *Eco*, Issue 10
Has American Government Gotten Too
Big? *Soc*, Issue 12
Is Involuntary Commitment Wrong?
Bio, Issue 9
Is the Widespread Use of Pesticides
Required to Feed the World's People?
Env, Issue 9
Should Compulsory Schooling Be
Abolished? *Edu*, Issue 7
Should Regulation of Airborne Toxins
Under the Clean Air Act Be
Strengthened? *Env*, Issue 7
Should The Federal Government
Deregulate American Business? *Eco*,
Issue 6
Should We Deregulate the Blood-
Banking Industry? *Eco*, Issue 3

Government spending
Can Federal Budget Deficits Be Good
for the Economy? *Eco*, Issue 14
Do U.S. Allies Share the Defense
Burden Fairly? *WP*, Issue 2
Is Incapacitation the Answer to the
Crime Problem? *Soc*, Issue 15
Is Mainstreaming Beneficial to All? *Edu*,
Issue 17
Is the United States in a Period of
Decline? *AH2*, Issue 16
Should Health Care for the Elderly Be
Limited? *Bio*, Issue 19
Should Immigration Be More Limited?
Soc, Issue 16
Should We Send Convicts to Penal
Colonies? *CR*, Issue 16

Was Dwight Eisenhower a Great
President? *AH2*, Issue 13
Gross National Product. *See* **GNP**
Groundwater. *See* **Water shortage**
Growth rate. *See* **Economic growth**
Gun control
Should Handguns Be Banned? *Leg*,
Issue 16
Will Gun Control Reduce Crime? *CR*,
Issue 15

— H —

Handguns. *See* **Gun Control**
Handicapism
Is Mainstreaming Beneficial to All? *Edu*,
Issue 17
Should Newborns Without Brains Be
Used as Organ Donors? *Bio*, Issue 16
Should Parents Be Allowed to Decide to
Withhold Treatment From Newborns
with Birth Defects? *Bio*, Issue 7

Hazardous waste
Are Environmentalists and Industrial
Leaders Becoming Less Adversarial?
Env, Issue 5
Hazardous Waste: Can Present
Regulatory and Voluntary Efforts
Solve Disposal and Clean-up
Problems? *Env*, Issue 13
Is Nuclear Deterrence Irrational? *Soc*,
Issue 17
Municipal Waste: Is Modern
Incineration Technology an
Environmentally Benign Alternative to
Garbage Dumps? *Env*, Issue 14
Nuclear Waste: Was Yucca Mountain an
Appropriate Site for Nuclear Waste
Disposal? *Env*, Issue 15
Should Regulation of Airborne Toxins
Under the Clean Air Act Be
Strengthened? *Env*, Issue 7

Health care
Are There Limits to Confidentiality?
Bio, Issue 8
Are School-Based Health Clinics an
Effective Way of Reducing Teenage
Pregnancies and STDs? *HS*, Issue 8
Do Diagnostic Labels Hinder the
Effective Treatment of Persons With
Mental Disorders? *Psy*, Issue 13

Does Risk-Benefit Analysis Provide an Objective Method for Making Environmental Decisions? *Env*, Issue 4

Do Patients Have a Right to Die? *Leg*, Issue 13

Do We Have a Moral Right to Die? *Mor*, Issue 6

Hazardous Waste: Can Present Regulatory and Voluntary Efforts Solve Disposal and Clean-up Problems? *Env*, Issue 13

Is Abortion Always Immoral? *Mor*, Issue 8

Is It Ethical to Implant Animal Hearts in Humans? *Bio*, Issue 12

Is "Killing" the Same as "Letting Die"? *Bio*, Issue 5

Is It Ethical to Withhold the Truth From Dying Patients? *Bio*, Issue 4

Is Psychotherapy Effective? *Psy*, Issue 15

Municipal Waste: Is Modern Incineration Technology an Environmentally Benign Alternative to Garbage Dumps? *Env*, Issue 14

Must Fluids and Nutrition Always Be Given To Dying Patients? *Bio*, Issue 6

Should Doctors Cut Costs at the Bedside? *Bio*, Issue 10

Should Health Care for the Elderly Be Limited? *Bio*, Issue 19

Should Insurance Companies Be Allowed to Screen for Antibodies to the AIDS Virus? *Bio*, Issue 18

Should Organ Procurement Be Based on Voluntarism? *Bio*, Issue 15

Should Parents Be Allowed to Decide to Withhold Treatment From Newborns with Birth Defects? *Bio*, Issue 7

Herbicides. *See* **Toxic chemicals**

Heredity. *See* **Genetics**

Homosexuality

Are Homosexual and Bisexual Relations Natural and Normal? *HS*, Issue 3

Are Homosexual Relations Deviant? *Soc*, Issue 14

Does Government Have a Constitutional Right to Prohibit Certain Kinds of Sexual Conduct? *HS*, Issue 14

Does Government Have a Right to Prohibit Homosexual Acts? *Pol*, Issue 15

Is It Unconstitutional to Discriminate Against Homosexuals? *Leg*, Issue 7

Should Our Society Recognize Nonmarital and Gay Unions? *HS*, Issue 16

Should the Law Enforce Morality? *Mor*, Issue 13

Will AIDS Become a Middle-Class Heterosexual Disease? *HS*, Issue 10

Human development

Does Behavioral Control Provide the Best Learning Environment? *Edu*, Issue 6

Is Abortion Always Immoral? *Mor*, Issue 8

Is Morality Relative? *Mor*, Issue 1

Is the Antiabortion Movement Based on a Belief in the Sacredness of Human Life? *HS*, Issue 11

Is the Control of Human Behavior a Proper Goal for Psychology? *Psy*, Issue 19

Should Schooling Be Based on Students' Social Experiences? *Edu*, Issue 1

Should Schooling Determine What Is Learned? *Edu*, Issue 2

Human rights. *See also* **Civil rights**

Are Homosexual Relations Deviant? *Soc*, Issue 14

Does Government Have a Constitutional Right to Prohibit Certain Kinds of Sexual Conduct? *HS*, Issue 14

Is Abortion Immoral? *Bio*, Issue 1

Is Involuntary Commitment Wrong? *Bio*, Issue 9

Should Morality and Human Rights Strongly Influence Foreign Policymaking? *WP*, Issue 15

Should Parents Be Allowed to Decide to Withhold Treatment From Newborns with Birth Defects? *Bio*, Issue 7

Should Schools Determine What Is Learned? *Edu*, Issue 2

Should There Be a Market in Body Parts? *Bio*, Issue 17

Was Abraham Lincoln America's Greatest President? *AH1*, Issue 16

— I —

Immigration
Is Bilingual Education Justifiable as a Policy? *Edu,* Issue 19
Should Immigration Be More Limited? *Soc,* Issue 16
Was Colonial American Culture Unique? *AH1,* Issue 1
Were the Immigrants' Old World Cultures Destroyed as They Adjusted to American Life? *AH2,* Issue 4

Income distribution
Is Economic Inequality Beneficial to Society? *Soc,* Issue 8
Is the Middle Class Shrinking? *Eco,* Issue 19
Is The Welfare System Causing Poverty? *Eco,* Issue 13

Income taxes. *See* **Tax structure**

Indians, American *See* **Native Americans**

Industrial policy
Are Profits the Only Business of Business? *Eco,* Issue 1, *Mor,* Issue 15
Is Street Crime More Serious Than White-Collar Crime? *CR,* Issue 4

Industry. *See also* **specific industry**
Are Environmentalists and Industrial Leaders Becoming Less Adversarial? *Env,* Issue 5
Are Profits the Only Business of Business? *Eco,* Issue 1, *Mor,* Issue 15
Are There Too Many Hostile Takeovers? *Eco,* Issue 5
Did the Progressives Fail? *AH2,* Issue 7
Did Women Achieve Greater Autonomy in the New Nation? *AH1,* Issue 9
Does an Elite Rule America? *Soc,* Issue 11
Does the Government Regulate Too Much? *Pol,* Issue 8
Do Firms Exploit Workers and Local Communities By Closing Profitable Plants? *Eco,* Issue 7
Hazardous Waste: Can Present Regulatory and Voluntary Efforts Solve Disposal and Clean-up Problems? *Env,* Issue 13
Is America Ruled by an Elite? *Pol,* Issue 1

Is Immediate Action Necessary to Minimize Potential Catastrophic Effects of Global Climatic Warming? *Env,* Issue 17
Is Immediate Action Needed to Combat the Effects of Acid Rain? *Env,* Issue 11
Is It Time to Abolish the Minimum Wage? *Eco,* Issue 9
Is Manufacturing Alive and Well and Living in the U.S.? *Eco,* Issue 20
Is Population Control the Key to Preventing Environmental Deterioration? *Env,* Issue 6
Is Street Crime More Serious Than White-Collar Crime? *CR,* Issue 4
Is the Environment Improving? *Soc,* Issue 19
Is There a Cancer Epidemic Due to Industrial Chemicals in the Environment? *Env,* Issue 10
Is the United States in a Period of Decline? *AH2,* Issue 16

Should Insurance Companies Be Allowed to Screen for Antibodies to the AIDS Virus? *Bio,* Issue 18
Should Regulation of Airborne Toxins Under the Clean Air Act Be Strengthened? *Env,* Issue 7
Should Schools Serve National Economic Needs? *Edu,* Issue 8
Should The Federal Government Deregulate American Business? *Eco,* Issue 6
Should There Be a Market in Body Parts? *Bio,* Issue 17
Should the United States Protect Domestic Industries from Foreign Competition? *Eco,* Issue 16
Should We Deregulate the Blood Banking Industry? *Eco,* Issue 3
Should We Try to Save the Family Farm? *Eco,* Issue 2
Should Women Be Excluded from Jobs That Could Be Hazardous to a Fetus? *Env,* Issue 12

Was City Government in Late Nineteenth-Century America a "Conspicuous Failure"? *AH2,* Issue 6
Was John D. Rockefeller a "Robber Baron"? *AH2,* Issue 2
Was the American Labor Movement Radical? *AH2,* Issue 3

Was the New Deal an Effective Answer to the Great Depression? *AH2*, Issue 11

Were the Immigrants' Old World Cultures Destroyed as They Adjusted to American Life? *AH2*, Issue 4

Were the Populists Democratic Reformers? *AH2*, Issue 5

Inequality

Did the Progressives Fail? *AH2*, Issue 7

Does "Lower-Class" Culture Perpetuate Poverty? *Soc*, Issue 2

Does Society Have an Obligation to Care for the Less Well Off? *Mor*, Issue 16

Does Tracking Support Educational Inequality? *Edu*, Issue 18

Is "Comparable Worth" Worthless? *Eco*, Issue 4

Is Economic Inequality Beneficial to Society? *Soc*, Issue 8

Should Workers Be Paid According to "Comparable Worth"? *Pol*, Issue 13

Insanity. *See* **Mental illness**

Insanity defense. *See also* **Crime**

Should Insanity Be Considered a Legal Defense for Criminals? *Psy*, Issue 18

Should the Insanity Defense Be Abolished? *Leg*, Issue 17

Intelligence. *See also* **Learning**

Can Intelligence Be Increased? *Psy*, Issue 11

Can Intelligence Be Measured with a Single Score? *Psy*, Issue 12

Should Parents Provide Academic Instruction for Their Children Before They're Old Enough for School? *Psy*, Issue 10

Intelligence Quotient (IQ). *See* **Intelligence**

Interest groups

Do Political Action Committees Undermine Democracy? *Pol*, Issue 3

Should Congress Be Reformed? *Pol*, Issue 5

International economy

Can Monetary and Fiscal Policies Still Be Used to Solve Our Macroeconomic Problems? *Eco*, Issue 11

Do U.S. Allies Share the Defense Burden Fairly? *WP*, Issue 2

Is America Declining? *Pol*, Issue 20

Is the Pain and Suffering Associated with Disinvestment and Sanctions Worth It for Black South African Workers? *Eco*, Issue 18

Is the United States Becoming Too Friendly with China? *WP*, Issue 1

Should Strict Sanctions Be Applied Against South Africa? *WP*, Issue 4

Should the United States Protect Domestic Industries from Foreign Competition? *Eco*, Issue 16

Will the Third World Pay Its Debt? *Eco*, Issue 17

International law

International Law: Should the United States Expel the PLO's Mission to the United Nations? *WP*, Issue 17

Is the United Nations a Beneficial Organization? *WP*, Issue 18

International relations

Can Military Action Reduce International Terrorism? *WP*, Issue 14

Could NATO Forces Withstand a Conventional Attack by the Warsaw Pact? *WP*, Issue 12

Did Woodrow Wilson Fail as Commander-in-Chief During World War I? *AH2*, Issue 9

Does the Soviet Union Truly Want International Cooperation? *WP*, Issue 6

Do Foreign Investments Threaten U.S. Economic Independence? *WP*, Issue 9

Is the United States a Declining Power? *WP*, Issue 7

Is the United States in a Period of Decline? *AH2*, Issue 16

Should Israel Agree to the Creation of a Palestinian State? *WP*, Issue 5

Should Morality and Human Rights Strongly Influence Foreign Policymaking? *WP*, Issue 15

Was the Conflict Between the United States and Russia Inevitable? *AH2*, Issue 12

Will the Canada-U.S. Free Trade Agreement Be Beneficial? *WP*, Issue 8

International trade. *See* **Trade**

Interpersonal relationships

Is the "New Woman" the Main Cause of Turmoil and Tension in Male/Female Relations Today? *HS*, Issue 2

"New Woman," The: Has She Confused Sex Roles? *Soc*, Issue 7

Should Curricula Emphasize
Commonality Over Diversity? *Edu*,
Issue 3
Should Schooling Be Based on
Students' Social Experience? *Edu*,
Issue 1

In vitro fertilization
Is It Wrong to Create Test-Tube Babies?
Bio, Issue 2
Should Research With Aborted Fetal
Tissue Be Banned? *Psy*, Issue 13

— J —

Jefferson, Thomas
Did President Jefferson Outfederalize
the Federalists? *AH1*, Issue 8
Has American Government Gotten Too
Big? *Soc*, Issue 12

Jobs. *See* **Employment; Unemployment**

Judicial system
Does the Supreme Court Abuse Its
Power? *Pol*, Issue 9
Do Patients Have a Right to Die? *Leg*,
Issue 13
Is It Unconstitutional to Discriminate
Against Homosexuals? *Leg*, Issue 7
Is the Legal Profession Declining? *Leg*,
Issue 5
Is There a Litigation Crisis? *Leg*, Issue 2
Should Lawyers Use "Hardball"
Tactics? *CR*, Issue 11
Should Plea Bargaining Be Abolished?
Leg, Issue 3
Should Pornography Be Protected by
the First Amendment? *Leg*, Issue 10
Should Surrogate Motherhood Contracts
Be Illegal? *Leg*, Issue 12
Should the Adversary System Be
Abolished? *Leg*, Issue 1
Should the Exclusionary Rule Be
Abolished? *Leg*, Issue 15
Should the Insanity Defense Be
Abolished? *Leg*, Issue 17
Should There Be a Right to Abortion?
Leg, Issue 9
Should Women Be Allowed to Bear
Babies for a Fee? *Bio*, Issue 3

Juvenile crime
Has the Women's Movement Increased
Female Criminality? *CR*, Issue 7

Juvenile Justice: Are Kids "Getting
Away With Murder"? *CR*, Issue 10

— K —

Kinship. *See* **Family structure;
Marriage**

— L —

Labor force
Can Women Combine Careers and
Families? *Soc*, Issue 6
Did Women Achieve Greater Autonomy
in the New Nations? *AH1*, Issue 9
Does Tracking Support Educational
Inequality? *Edu*, Issue 18
Do Firms Exploit Workers and Local
Communities By Closing Profitable
Plants? *Eco*, Issue 7
Is "Comparable Worth" Worthless? *Eco*,
Issue 4
Is It Time to Abolish the Minimum
Wage? *Eco*, Issue 9
Should Congress Guarantee U.S.
Workers the Right to Parental Leave?
Eco, Issue 8
Should Women Be Excluded from Jobs
That Could Be Hazardous to a Fetus?
Env, Issue 12
Should Workers Be Paid According to
"Comparable Worth"? *Pol*, Issue 13
Was the American Labor Movement
Radical? *AH2*, Issue 3

Latin America
Is American Intervention in Latin
America Justified? *Pol*, Issue 18
Is U.S. Intervention in Latin America
and Elsewhere Justified? *WP*, Issue 3
Should Morality and Human Rights
Strongly Influence Foreign
Policymaking? *WP*, Issue 15
Should the Less Developed Countries
Pay Their International Debts? *WP*,
Issue 11
Was U.S. Intervention in Nicaragua in
the Early Twentieth Century Motivated
by "Dollar Diplomacy"? *AH2*, Issue 8
Will the Third World Pay Its Debt? *Eco*,
Issue 17

Law enforcement. *See also* **Crime prevention**
Are Official Statistics Meaningful? *CR*, Issue 5
Does Risk-Benefit Analysis Provide an Objective Method for Making Environmental Decisions? *Env*, Issue 4
Do We Need More Jails? *CR*, Issue 14
Do We Need More Stringently Enforced Regulations to Protect Endangered Species? *Env*, Issue 2
International Law: Should the United States Expel the PLO's Mission to the United Nations? *WP*, Issue 17
Is Crime Created by Society's Elites? *CR*, Issue 2
Is the Criminal Justice System Racist? *CR*, Issue 8
Should Prostitution Be Decriminalized? *HS*, Issue 17
Should the Exclusionary Rule Be Abolished? *Leg*, Issue 15
Should the Law Enforce Morality? *Mor*, Issue 13
Should the Police Do More to Manage Street Life? *Leg*, Issue 4
Will Tougher Sentencing Reduce Crime? *Pol*, Issue 10

Law enforcement officers. *See* **Police**

Law of the Sea. *See* **International law**

Lawyers
Is the Legal Profession Declining? *Leg*, Issue 5
Is There a Litigation Crisis? *Leg*, Issue 2
Should Insanity Be Considered a Legal Defense for Criminals? *Psy*, Issue 18
Should Lawyers Use "Hardball" Tactics? *CR*, Issue 11
Should Plea Bargaining Be Abolished? *Leg*, Issue 3
Should the Adversary System Be Abolished? *Leg*, Issue 1

Learning
Are Packaged Discipline Programs Harmful? *Edu*, Issue 16
Are Specific Programs to Teach Thinking Needed? *Edu*, Issue 13
Can Intelligence Be Increased? *Psy*, Issue 11
Can Intelligence Be Measured with a Single Score? *Psy*, Issue 12
Does Behavioral Control Provide the Best Learning Environment? *Edu*, Issue 6
Is Bilingual Education Justifiable as a Policy? *Edu*, Issue 19
Is Mainstreaming Beneficial to All? *Edu*, Issue 17
Is Measurement-Driven Instruction Desirable? *Edu*, Issue 15
Must All Students Be Given the Same Kind of Schooling? *Edu*, Issue 10
Should Children Learn Morality Primarily by Examining Their Own Reasoning? *Psy*, Issue 9
Should Compulsory Schooling Be Abolished? *Edu*, Issue 7
Should Curricula Emphasize Commonality Over Diversity? *Edu*, Issue 3
Should Parents Provide Academic Instruction for Their Children Before They're Old Enough for School? *Psy*, Issue 10
Should Schools Determine What Is Learned? *Edu*, Issue 2
Should Very Young Children Receive Academic Instruction? *Edu*, Issue 12

Legislation
Abortion: Should Public Officials Protect The "Right to Choose"? *Pol*, Issue 16
Does Risk-Benefit Analysis Provide an Objective Method for Making Environmental Decisions? *Env*, Issue 4
Does the Government Regulate Too Much? *Pol*, Issue 8
Does Wilderness Have Intrinsic Value? *Env*, Issue 1
Do We Need More Stringently Enforced Regulations to Protect Endangered Species? *Env*, Issue 2
Do We Need New Federal Legislation to Protect the Future Integrity of Our Groundwater? *Env*, Issue 16
Is "Comparable Worth" Worthless? *Eco*, Issue 4
Is Crime Created by Society's Elites? *CR*, Issue 2
Is Immediate Action Needed to Combat the Effects of Acid Rain? *Env*, Issue 11
Is Mainstreaming Beneficial to All? *Edu*, Issue 17

Is Tax Reform an Impossible Dream
Come True? *Eco*, Issue 12
Should Capital Punishment Be
Abolished? *CR*, Issue 13, *Mor*, Issue 11
Should Congress Be Reformed? *Pol*,
Issue 5
Should Handguns Be Banned? *Leg*,
Issue 16
Should Prostitution Be Decriminalized?
HS, Issue 17
Should Regulation of Airborne Toxins
Under the Clean Air Act Be
Strengthened? *Env*, Issue 7
Should the Death Penalty Be
Abolished? *Leg*, Issue 14
Should the U.S. Congress Limit the
President's War Powers? *WP*, Issue 16
Should We Deregulate the Blood-
Banking Industry? *Eco*, Issue 3
Should We Try to Save the Family
Farm? *Eco*, Issue 2
Was the New Deal an Effective Answer
to the Great Depression? *AH2*, Issue
11
Will Drug Legalization Help the
Criminal Justice System? *CR*, Issue 17

Liberalism
Do the News Media Have a Liberal
Bias? *Pol*, Issue 4
Has American Government Become Too
Big? *Eco*, Issue 10
Has American Government Gotten Too
Big? *Soc*, Issue 12
Should the Law Enforce Morality? *Mor*,
Issue 13

Life expectancy
Is the Environment Improving? *Soc*,
Issue 19
Should Health Care for the Elderly Be
Limited? *Bio*, Issue 19

Lincoln, Abraham
Can the Revolution Serve as a
Developmental Model for Third World
Nations Today? *AH1*, Issue 6
Was Abraham Lincoln America's
Greatest President? *AH1*, Issue 16

Lobbyists. *See* **Interest groups**

Lobotomy. *See* **Mental illness**

Local government
Constitution, The: Was It an Economic
Document? *AH1*, Issue 7

Does Government Have a Right to
Prohibit Homosexual Acts? *Pol*,
Issue 15
Hazardous Waste: Can Present
Regulatory and Voluntary Efforts
Solve Disposal and Clean-up
Problems? *Env*, Issue 13
Should the Police Direct Community
Crime Prevention? *CR*, Issue 9
Was City Government in Late
Nineteenth-Century America a
"Conspicuous Failure"? *AH2*, Issue 6

Lower class
Does "Lower-Class" Culture Perpetuate
Poverty? *Soc*, Issue 2
Does Welfare Do More Harm Than
Good? *Soc*, Issue 13
Is the Welfare System Causing Poverty?
Eco, Issue 13
Was Antebellum Reform Motivated
Primarily by Humanitarian Goals?
AH1, Issue 11
Was the Antebellum South a Unique
Section in American History? *AH1*,
Issue 15

— M —

Marriage
Did Slavery Destroy the Black Family?
AH1, Issue 13
Does Good Sex Require Love? *HS*,
Issue 4
Is Extramarital Sex Wrong? *Mor*, Issue 9
Is Monogamy the Best Form of
Marriage? *HS*, Issue 5
Is Sex Education in Schools an Attempt
to Institutionalize a Sexual Revolution?
HS, Issue 7
Is The Sexual Revolution Over? *HS*,
Issue 1
Should Our Society Recognize
Nonmarital and Gay Unions? *HS*,
Issue 16
Should the State Require All Family
Life Education Programs to Stress
Premarital Chastity and Monogamy?
HS, Issue 15

Media. *See also* **Television**
Can Military Action Reduce
International Terrorism? *WP*, Issue 14

Do the News Media Have a Liberal Bias? *Pol*, Issue 4

Have American Political Parties Lost Their Power? *Pol*, Issue 2

Should Morality and Human Rights Strongly Influence Foreign Policymaking? *WP*, Issue 15

Should Pornography Be Protected by the First Amendment? *Leg*, Issue 10

Should We Examine the Private Lives of Presidential Candidates? *Pol*, Issue 6

Will AIDS Become a Middle-Class Heterosexual Disease? *HS*, Issue 10

Medical care. *See* **Health care**

Medical costs

Has American Government Gotten Too Big? *Soc*, Issue 12

Should Doctors Cut Costs at the Bedside? *Bio*, Issue 10

Memory

Should Electroshock Therapy Be Discontinued? *Psy*, Issue 16

Should Very Young Children Receive Academic Instruction? *Edu*, Issue 12

Mental health

Do Attitudes Affect Cancer? *Psy*, Issue 4

Should Insanity Be Considered a Legal Defense for Criminals? *Psy*, Issue 18

Should the Insanity Defense Be Abolished? *Leg*, Issue 17

Mental illness

Can Suicide Be Rational? *Psy*, Issue 14

Do Diagnostic Labels Hinder the Effective Treatment of Persons With Mental Disorders? *Psy*, Issue 13

Is Involuntary Commitment Wrong? *Bio*, Issue 9

Is Psychotherapy Effective? *Psy*, Issue 15

Should Electroshock Therapy Be Discontinued? *Psy*, Issue 16

Should Insanity Be Considered a Legal Defense for Criminals? *Psy*, Issue 18

Should the Insanity Defense Be Abolished? *Leg*, Issue 17

Should the Use of the Principles of Conditioning Be Limited in the Modification of Undesirable Behavior? *Psy*, Issue 7

Mexico. *See also* **Latin America**

Should the Less Developed Countries Pay Their International Debts? *WP*, Issue 11

Will the Third World Pay Its Debt? *Eco*, Issue 17

Middle class

Is the Middle Class Shrinking? *Eco*, Issue 19

Was Antebellum Reform Motivated Primarily by Humanitarian Goals? *AH1*, Issue 11

Will AIDS Become a Middle-Class Heterosexual Disease? *HS*, Issue 10

Middle East

Can Military Action Reduce International Terrorism? *WP*, Issue 14

International Law: Should the United States Expel the PLO's Mission to the United Nations? *WP*, Issue 17

Should Israel Agree to the Creation of a Palestinian State? *WP*, Issue 5

Migration. *See* **Immigration**

Military

Can Military Action Reduce International Terrorism? *WP*, Issue 14

Could NATO Forces Withstand a Conventional Attack by the Warsaw Pact? *WP*, Issue 12

Could the United States Have Prevented the Fall of South Vietnam? *AH2*, Issue 14

Did Woodrow Wilson Fail as Commander-in-Chief During World War I? *AH2*, Issue 9

Does Morality Require Nuclear Disarmament? *Mor*, Issue 18

Does the Soviet Union Truly Want International Cooperation? *WP*, Issue 6

Do U.S. Allies Share the Defense Burden Fairly? *WP*, Issue 2

Has Congress Restricted Presidential War Powers Too Much? *Pol*, Issue 7

Is America Declining? *Pol*, Issue 20

Is American Intervention in Latin America Justified? *Pol*, Issue 18

Is The United States a Declining Power? *WP*, Issue 7

Is the United States in a Period of Decline? *AH2*, Issue 16

Should Superpower Strategic Arsenals Be Cut in Half? *WP*, Issue 13

Should the U.S. Congress Limit the President's War Powers? *WP*, Issue 16

Was Abraham Lincoln America's Greatest President? *AH1*, Issue 16

Was the Conflict Between the United States and Russia Inevitable? *AH2*, Issue 12

Was U.S. Intervention in Nicaragua in the Early Twentieth Century Motivated by "Dollar Diplomacy"? *AH2*, Issue 8

Was Reconstruction a Total Failure? *AH1*, Issue 17, *AH2*, Issue 1

Was U.S. Foreign Policy in the Early Nineteenth Century Imperialistic? *AH1*, Issue 12

Minorities

Does Our Welfare System Hurt the Poor? *Pol*, Issue 14

Does Society Have an Obligation to Care for the Less Well Off? *Mor*, Issue 16

Does Tracking Support Educational Inequality? *Edu*, Issue 18

Is Affirmative Action Constitutional? *Leg*, Issue 11

Is Affirmative Action Morally Justified? *Mor*, Issue 14

Is Affirmative Action Reverse Discrimination? *Pol*, Issue 12, *Soc*, Issue 10

Is Bilingual Education Justifiable as a Policy? *Edu*, Issue 19

Should Curricula Emphasize Commonality Over Diversity? *Edu*, Issue 3

Should Workers Be Paid According to "Comparable Worth"? *Pol*, Issue 13

Was Martin Luther King, Jr.'s Leadership Essential to the Success of the Civil Rights Movement? *AH2*, Issue 15

Will AIDS Become a Middle-Class Heterosexual Disease? *HS*, Issue 10

Monetary policy

Can Monetary and Fiscal Policies Still Be Used to Solve Our Macroeconomic Problems? *Eco*, Issue 11

Did Monetary Policy Cause the Stock Market Crash in 1987? *Eco*, Issue 15

Money supply

Can Monetary and Fiscal Policies Still Be Used to Solve Our Macroeconomic Problems? *Eco*, Issue 11

Did Monetary Policy Cause the Stock Market Crash of 1987? *Eco*, Issue 15

Is Tax Reform an Impossible Dream Come True? *Eco*, Issue 12

Moral issues *See* **Ethical issues**

Mothering. *See also* **Fathering; Parenting**

Can Women Combine Careers and Families? *Soc*, Issue 6

Did Slavery Destroy the Black Family? *AH1*, Issue 13

Do Surrogate Motherhood Contracts Exploit Women? *HS*, Issue 18

Should Surrogate Motherhood Contracts Be Illegal? *Leg*, Issue 12

Should Women Be Allowed to Bear Babies for a Fee? *Bio*, Issue 3

— N —

Native Americans

Was Colonial American Culture Unique? *AH1*, Issue 1

Was Conflict Unavoidable Between Native Americans and Colonists? *AH1*, Issue 2

Natural resources

Are Abundant Resources and an Improved Environment Likely Future Prospects for the World's People? *Env*, Issue 19

Does Wilderness Have Intrinsic Value? *Env*, Issue 1

Is EPA's Strategy Evolving to Meet Present and Future Environmental Problems? *Env*, Issue 3

Negroes. *See* **Blacks**

Neurosis. *See* **Mental illness**

News media. *See* **Media**

Nuclear arms race. *See* **Nuclear weapons**

Nuclear energy

Is Nuclear Power Safe and Desirable? *Env*, Issue 8

Nuclear Waste: Was Yucca Mountain an Appropriate Site for Nuclear Waste Disposal? *Env*, Issue 15

Nuclear war

Could NATO Forces Withstand a Conventional Attack by the Warsaw Pact? *WP*, Issue 12

Does Morality Require Nuclear Disarmament? *Mor*, Issue 18

Is Nuclear Deterrence Irrational? *Soc*, Issue 17

Should Superpower Strategic Arsenals Be Cut in Half? *WP*, Issue 13

Nuclear waste. *See* **Hazardous waste**

Nuclear weapons
Could NATO Forces Withstand a Conventional Attack by the Warsaw Pact? *WP*, Issue 12
Does Morality Require Nuclear Disarmament? *Mor*, Issue 18
Is Nuclear Deterrence Irrational? *Soc*, Issue 17
Is Nuclear Power Safe and Desirable? *Env*, Issue 8
Should Superpower Strategic Arsenals Be Cut in Half? *WP*, Issue 13
Was Dwight Eisenhower a Great President? *AH2*, Issue 13

— O —

Overpopulation. *See* **Population growth**

Ozone
Does the Montreal Ozone Agreement Signal a New Era of International Environmental Statesmanship? *Env*, Issue 18
Is Immediate Action Necessary to Minimize Potential Catastrophic Effects of Global Climatic Warming? *Env*, Issue 17
Is the World Climate Threatened by Global Warming? *WP*, Issue 19

— P —

PACS
Do Political Action Committees Undermine Democracy? *Pol*, Issue 3
Is America Ruled by an Elite? *Eco*, Issue 1

Parenting. *See also* **Fathering; Mothering**
Are Traditional Families More Successful? *Soc*, Issue 5
Can Women Combine Careers and Families? *Soc*, Issue 6
Did Slavery Destroy the Black Family? *AH1*, Issue 13

Do Surrogate Motherhood Contracts Exploit Women? *HS*, Issue 18
Should Congress Guarantee U.S. Workers the Right to Parental Leave? *Eco*, Issue 8
Should Surrogate Motherhood Contracts Be Illegal? *Leg*, Issue 12
Should Women Be Allowed to Bear Babies for a Fee? *Bio*, Issue 3

Pesticides. *See* **Toxic chemicals**

Pill, The. *See* **Birth control**

Police. *See also* **Crime**
Do We Need More Jails? *CR*, Issue 14
Should the Exclusionary Rule Be Abolished? *Leg*, Issue 15
Should the Police Direct Community Crime Prevention? *CR*, Issue 9
Should the Police Do More to Manage Street Life? *Leg*, Issue 4

Political Action Committees. *See* **PACS**

Political campaigns. *See* **Campaigns, political**

Political history, Colonial
Can the Revolution Serve as a Developmental Model for Third World Nations Today? *AH1*, Issue 6
Was the Great Awakening a Key to the American Revolution? *AH1*, Issue 5

Political history, Post–Civil War
Was City Government in Late Nineteenth-Century America a "Conspicuous Failure"? *AH2*, Issue 6
Was Reconstruction a Total Failure? *AH1*, Issue 17, *AH2*, Issue 1
Were the Populists Democratic Reformers? *AH2*, Issue 5

Political history, Pre–Civil War
Constitution, The: Was It an Economic Document? *AH1*, Issue 7
Did President Jefferson Outfederalize the Federalists? *AH1*, Issue 8
Did the Election of 1828 Represent a Democratic Revolt of the People? *AH1*, Issue 10
Was the Antebellum South a Unique Section in American History? *AH1*, Issue 15
Were the Abolitionists "Unrestrained Fanatics?" *AH1*, Issue 14

Political history, Twentieth Century
Did the Progressives Fail? *AH2*, Issue 7

Did the Women's Movement Die in the 1920s? *AH2*, Issue 10

Was Dwight Eisenhower a Great President? *AH2*, Issue 13

Was U.S. Intervention in Nicaragua in the Early Twentieth Century Motivated by "Dollar Diplomacy"? *AH2*, Issue 8

Political parties

Did President Jefferson Outfederalize the Federalists? *AH1*, Issue 8

Did the Election of 1828 Represent a Democratic Revolt of the People? *AH1*, Issue 10

Did the Progressives Fail? *AH2*, Issue 7

Have American Political Parties Lost Their Power? *Pol*, Issue 2

Political philosophy

Did President Jefferson Outfederalize the Federalists? *AH1*, Issue 8

Does Morality Require Nuclear Disarmament? *Mor*, Issue 18

Do Rich Nations Have an Obligation to Help Poor Nations? *Mor*, Issue 17

Political systems

Should Israel Agree to the Creation of a Palestinian State? *WP*, Issue 5

Was City Government in Late Nineteenth-Century America a "Conspicuous Failure"? *AH2*, Issue 6

Pollution. *See also* **Hazardous waste; Toxic chemicals; Water pollution**

Are Abundant Resources and an Improved Environment Likely Future Prospects for the World's People? *Env*, Issue 19

Are Environmentalists and Industrial Leaders Becoming Less Adversarial? *Env*, Issue 5

Does Risk-Benefit Analysis Provide an Objective Method for Making Environmental Decisions? *Env*, Issue 4

Do We Need New Federal Legislation to Protect the Future Integrity of Our Groundwater? *Env*, Issue 16

Is the Environment Improving? *Soc*, Issue 19

Is the World Climate Threatened by Global Warming? *WP*, Issue 19

Is Urban Life Crazy? *Soc*, Issue 4

Municipal Waste: Is Modern Incineration Technology an Environmentally Benign Alternative to Garbage Dumps? *Env*, Issue 14

Should Regulation of Airborne Toxins Under the Clean Air Act Be Strengthened? *Env*, Issue 7

Poor. *See* **Poverty**

Population growth

Are Abundant Resources and an Improved Environment Likely Future Prospects for the World's People? *Env*, Issue 19

Do Rich Nations Have an Obligation to Help Poor Nations? *Mor*, Issue 17

Is Population Control the Key to Preventing Environmental Deterioration? *Env*, Issue 6

Is the Environment Improving? *Soc*, Issue 19

Is the Widespread Use of Pesticides Required to Feed the World's People? *Env*, Issue 9

Is the World Threatened by a Population Bomb? *Soc*, Issue 18

Should Immigration Be More Limited? *Soc*, Issue 16

Was City Government in Late Nineteenth-Century America a "Conspicuous Failure"? *AH2*, Issue 6

Pornography

Does Pornography Promote Sexual Violence? *HS*, Issue 13

Is Pornography a Threat to Society? *Mor*, Issue 12

Is Pornography Harmful? *Psy*, Issue 17

Should Pornography Be Protected by the First Amendment? *Leg*, Issue 10

Poverty

Does "Lower-Class" Culture Perpetuate Poverty? *Soc*, Issue 2

Does Our Welfare System Hurt the Poor? *Pol*, Issue 14

Does Society Have an Obligation to Care for the Less Well Off? *Mor*, Issue 16

Does Welfare Do More Harm Than Good? *Soc*, Issue 13

Do Rich Nations Have an Obligation to Help Poor Nations? *Mor*, Issue 17

Is Population Control the Key to Preventing Environmental Deterioration? *Env*, Issue 6

Is the Third World Responsible for Its Own Lack of Economic Development? *WP*, Issue 10

Is The Welfare System Causing Poverty? *Eco*, Issue 13

Should the Less Developed Countries Pay Their International Debts? *WP*, Issue 11

Was Antebellum Reform Motivated Primarily by Humanitarian Goals? *AH1*, Issue 11

Prejudice. *See* **Minorities; Racial discrimination; Sex discrimination; Women's issues**

Presidency. *See also* **names of specific presidents**

Could the United States Have Prevented the Fall of South Vietnam? *AH2*, Issue 14

Did President Jefferson Outfederalize the Federalists? *AH1*, Issue 8

Did the Election of 1828 Represent a Democratic Revolt of the People? *AH1*, Issue 10

Did Woodrow Wilson Fail as Commander-in-Chief During World War I? *AH2*, Issue 9

Has Congress Restricted Presidential War Powers Too Much? *Pol*, Issue 7

Should Congress Be Reformed? *Pol*, Issue 5

Should the U.S. Congress Limit the President's War Powers? *WP*, Issue 16

Should We Examine the Private Lives of Presidential Candidates? *Pol*, Issue 6

Was Abraham Lincoln America's Greatest President? *AH1*, Issue 16

Was Dwight Eisenhower a Great President? *AH2*, Issue 13

Press, The. *See* **Media**

Prohibition. *See* **Alcohol**

Psychological research

Can Deception in Research Be Justified? *Bio*, Issue 11

Is Pornography Harmful? *Psy*, Issue 17

Is Psychotherapy Effective? *Psy*, Issue 15

Is the Control of Human Behavior a Proper Goal for Psychology? *Psy*, Issue 19

Is the State of Hypnosis a Unique Altered State of Consciousness? *Psy*, Issue 6

Should the Use of the Principles of Conditioning Be Limited in the Modification of Undesirable Behavior? *Psy*, Issue 7

Does Welfare Do More Harm Than Good? *Soc*, Issue 13

Is Tax Reform an Impossible Dream Come True? *Eco*, Issue 12

Should The Federal Government Deregulate American Business? *Eco*, Issue 6

Recession

Did Monetary Policy Cause the Stock Market Crash of 1987? *Eco*, Issue 15

Should We Try to Save the Family Farm? *Eco*, Issue 2

Refugees. *See* **Immigration**

Regulation. *See* **Government regulation**

Rehabilitation

Do We Have a Moral Responsibility to Rehabilitate Criminals? *Mor*, Issue 10

Do We Need More Jails? *CR*, Issue 14

Is Selective Incapacitation Just? *CR*, Issue 12

Relationships, interpersonal. *See* **Interpersonal relationships**

Religion. *See also* **specific religion**

Abortion: Should Public Officials Protect The "Right to Choose"? *Pol*, Issue 16

Can Suicide Be Rational? *Psy*, Issue 14

Do the Ends Justify the Means? *Mor*, Issue 5

Is Church-State Separation Being Threatened? *Edu*, Issue 5

Is Morality Relative? *Mor*, Issue 1

Is Morality the Exclusive Province of Religion? *Mor*, Issue 3

Is the Antiabortion Movement Based on a Belief in the Sacredness of Human Life? *HS*, Issue 11

Should Israel Agree to the Creation of a Palestinian State? *WP*, Issue 5

Should One Always Follow One's Conscience? *Mor*, Issue 4

Should Our Society Recognize Nonmarital and Gay Unions? *HS*, Issue 16

Should Prayer Be Permitted in Public Schools? *Leg*, Issue 8

Should Prenatal Testing for Sex Selection Be Permitted? *HS*, Issue 9

Should There Be a Right to Abortion? *Leg*, Issue 9

Should Values Be Developed Rather Than Transmitted? *Edu*, Issue 4

Should We Have a "Wall of Separation" Between Church and State? *Pol,* Issue 17

Was Conflict Unavoidable Between Native Americans and Colonists? *AH1,* Issue 2

Was the Great Awakening a Key to the American Revolution? *AH1,* Issue 5

Republican party
Did the Election of 1828 Represent a Democratic Revolt of the People? *AH1,* Issue 10

Have American Political Parties Lost Their Power? *Pol,* Issue 2

Was Abraham Lincoln America's Greatest President? *AH1,* Issue 16

Was Dwight Eisenhower a Great President? *AH2,* Issue 13

Republic of South Africa. *See* **South Africa, Republic of**

Revolution. *See* **American Revolution**

Roman Catholic Church. *See* **Church, Roman Catholic**

Russia. *See* **Soviet Union**

— S —

SALT
Could NATO Forces Withstand a Conventional Attack by the Warsaw Pact? *WP,* Issue 12

Should Superpower Strategic Arsenals Be Cut in Half? *WP,* Issue 13

School reform
Are Proposed Elementary School Reforms Realistic? *Edu,* Issue 11

Are Tests of Teacher Knowledge Fair? *Edu,* Issue 20

Are the Cards Stacked Against True School Reform? *Edu,* Issue 9

Must All Students Be Given the Same Kind of Schooling? *Edu,* Issue 10

Should Compulsory Schooling Be Abolished? *Edu,* Issue 7

Should Schools Serve National Economic Needs? *Edu,* Issue 8

Schools
Are Packaged Discipline Programs Harmful? *Edu,* Issue 16

Are Proposed Elementary School Reforms Realistic? *Edu,* Issue 11

Are School-Based Health Clinics an Effective Way of Reducing Teenage Pregnancies and STDs? *HS,* Issue 8

Are Specific Programs to Teach Thinking Needed? *Edu,* Issue 13

Are Tests of Teacher Knowledge Fair? *Edu,* Issue 20

Are the Cards Stacked Against True School Reform? *Edu,* Issue 9

Does Behavioral Control Provide the Best Learning Environment? *Edu,* Issue 6

Does Tracking Support Educational Inequality? *Edu,* Issue 18

Is Church-State Separation Being Threatened? *Edu,* Issue 5

Is Mainstreaming Beneficial to All? *Edu,* Issue 17

Is Measurement-Driven Instruction Desirable? *Edu,* Issue 15

Is Sex Education in Schools an Attempt to Institutionalize a Sexual Revolution? *HS,* Issue 7

Must All Students Be Given the Same Kind of Schooling? *Edu,* Issue 10

Should Children Learn Morality Primarily by Examining Their Own Reasoning? *Psy,* Issue 9

Should Compulsory Schooling Be Abolished? *Edu,* Issue 7

Should Curricula Emphasize Commonality Over Diversity? *Edu,* Issue 3

Should Literacy Be Based on Traditional Culture? *Edu,* Issue 14

Should Prayer Be Permitted in Public Schools? *Leg,* Issue 8

Should Schooling Be Based on Students' Social Experiences? *Edu,* Issue 1

Should Schools Determine What Is Learned? *Edu,* Issue 2

Should Schools Serve National Economic Needs? *Edu,* Issue 8

Should the State Require All Family Life Education Programs to Stress Premarital Chastity and Monogamy? *HS,* Issue 15

Should Values Be Developed Rather Than Transmitted? *Edu,* Issue 4

Scientific research
Can Computers Think? *Psy,* Issue 8

Can Deception in Psychological Research Be Justified? *Psy*, Issue 1

Can Deception in Research Be Justified? *Bio*, Issue 11

Can Intelligence Be Increased? *Psy*, Issue 11

Can Intelligence Be Measured with a Single Score? *Psy*, Issue 12

Do Attitudes Affect Cancer? *Psy*, Issue 4

Does Risk-Benefit Analysis Provide an Objective Method for Making Environmental Decisions? *Env*, Issue 4

Has Science Discredited ESP? *Psy*, Issue 5

Is It Ethical to Implant Animal Hearts in Humans? *Bio*, Issue 12

Is It Ethical to Withhold the Truth From Dying Patients? *Bio*, Issue 4

Is It Wrong to Create Test-Tube Babies? *Bio*, Issue 2

Is It Wrong to "Politicize" Sociology? *Soc*, Issue 1

Is Morality Subjective? *Mor*, Issue 2

Is Psychotherapy Effective? *Psy*, Issue 15

Is the Control of Human Behavior a Proper Goal for Psychology? *Psy*, Issue 19

Is the State of Hypnosis a Unique Altered State of Consciousness? *Psy*, Issue 6

Should Animal Experimentation Be Permitted? *Bio*, Issue 14

Should Organ Procurement Be Based on Voluntarism? *Bio*, Issue 15

Should Research With Aborted Fetal Tissue Be Banned? *Bio*, Issue 13

Should There Be a Market in Body Parts? *Bio*, Issue 17

Self

Are the Cards Stacked Against True School Reform? *Edu*, Issue 9

Do Diagnostic Labels Hinder the Effective Treatment of Persons With Mental Disorders? *Psy*, Issue 13

Does Good Sex Require Love? *HS*, Issue 4

Does Tracking Support Educational Inequality? *Edu*, Issue 18

Has Individualism Become Excessive? *Soc*, Issue 3

Is Morality Subjective? *Mor*, Issue 2

Is Our Behavior Primarily Determined by Biological Processes? *Psy*, Issue 3

Should One Always Follow One's Conscience? *Mor*, Issue 4

Should Our Society Recognize Nonmarital and Gay Unions? *HS*, Issue 16

Should Parents Provide Academic Instruction for Their Children Before They're Old Enough for School? *Psy*, Issue 10

Sex discrimination

Are Homosexual Relations Deviant? *Soc*, Issue 14

Is Affirmative Action Morally Justified? *Mor*, Issue 14

Is "Comparable Worth" Worthless? *Pol*, Issue 4

Is Economic Inequality Beneficial to Society? *Soc*, Issue 8

Is It Unconstitutional to Discriminate Against Homosexuals? *Leg*, Issue 7

Should There Be a Right to Abortion? *Leg*, Issue 9

Should Workers Be Paid According to "Comparable Worth"? *Pol*, Issue 13

Was the Colonial Period a "Golden Age" for Women in America? *AH1*, Issue 3

Sex roles

Did Women Achieve Greater Autonomy in the New Nations? *AH1*, Issue 9

Is the "New Woman" the Main Cause of Turmoil and Tension in Male/Female Relations Today? *HS*, Issue 2

Is The Sexual Revolution Over? *HS*, Issue 1

"New Woman," The: Has She Confused Sex Roles? *Soc*, Issue 7

Was the Colonial Period a "Golden Age" for Women in America? *AH1*, Issue 3

Sexuality

Are School-Based Health Clinics an Effective Way of Reducing Teenage Pregnancies and STDs? *HS*, Issue 8

Can Sex Be an Addiction? *HS*, Issue 6

Does Good Sex Require Love? *HS*, Issue 4

Does Government Have a Constitutional Right to Prohibit Certain Kinds of Sexual Conduct? *HS*, Issue 14

Does Pornography Promote Sexual Violence? *HS*, Issue 13

Is Rape Motivated by Aggression Instead of Sex? *HS*, Issue 12

Is Sex Education in Schools an Attempt to Institutionalize a Sexual Revolution? *HS*, Issue 7

Should Our Society Recognize Nonmarital and Gay Unions? *HS*, Issue 16

Slavery

Did American Slaves Develop a Distinct Afro-American Culture in the Eighteenth Century? *AH1*, Issue 4

Did Slavery Destroy the Black Family? *AH1*, Issue 13

Was Abraham Lincoln America's Greatest President? *AH1*, Issue 16

Was the Antebellum South a Unique Section in American History? *AH1*, Issue 15

Were the Abolitionists "Unrestrained Fanatics"? *AH1*, Issue 14

Social change

Are Homosexual and Bisexual Relations Natural and Normal? *HS*, Issue 3

Can Sex Be an Addiction? *HS*, Issue 6

Can the Revolution Serve as a Developmental Model for Third World Nations Today? *AH1*, Issue 6

Did American Slaves Develop a Distinct Afro-American Culture in the Eighteenth Century? *AH1*, Issue 4

Did the Women's Movement Die in the 1920s? *AH2*, Issue 10

Did Women Achieve Greater Autonomy in the New Nations? *AH1*, Issue 9

Has the Women's Movement Increased Female Criminality? *CR*, Issue 7

Is Crime Functional? *CR*, Issue 1

Is Crime Getting Worse? *CR*, Issue 6

Is Extramarital Sex Wrong? *Mor*, Issue 9

Is Sex Education in Schools an Attempt to Institutionalize a Sexual Revolution? *HS*, Issue 7

Is the "New Woman" the Main Cause of Turmoil and Tension in Male/Female Relations Today? *HS*, Issue 2

Is There a Litigation Crisis? *Leg*, Issue 2

Is The Sexual Revolution Over? *HS*, Issue 1

"New Woman," The: Has She Confused Sex Roles? *Soc*, Issue 7

Should Our Society Recognize Nonmarital and Gay Unions? *HS*, Issue 16

Should Prenatal Testing for Sex Selection Be Permitted? *HS*, Issue 9

Should Very Young Children Receive Academic Instruction? *Edu*, Issue 12

Was Antebellum Reform Motivated Primarily by Humanitarian Goals? *AH1*, Issue 11

Was Colonial American Culture Unique? *AH1*, Issue 1

Was the American Labor Movement Radical? *AH2*, Issue 3

Was the Colonial Period a "Golden Age" for Women in America? *AH1*, Issue 3

Was the New Deal an Effective Answer to the Great Depression? *AH2*, Issue 11

Were the Immigrants' Old World Cultures Destroyed as They Adjusted to American Life? *AH2*, Issue 4

Were the Populists Democratic Reformers? *AH2*, Issue 5

Social class. *See* **Lower class; Social discrimination**

Social discrimination

Does Tracking Support Educational Inequality? *Edu*, Issue 18

Is Economic Inequality Beneficial to Society? *Soc*, Issue 8

Is Racial Oppression Declining in America? *Soc*, Issue 9

Should Literacy Be Based on Traditional Culture? *Edu*, Issue 14

Social history, Colonial

Was Colonial American Culture Unique? *AH1*, Issue 1

Was the Colonial Period a "Golden Age" for Women in America? *AH1*, Issue 3

Social history, Post–Civil War

Was Reconstruction a Total Failure? *AH1*, Issue 17, *AH2*, Issue 1

Social history, Pre–Civil War

Did Women Achieve Greater Autonomy in the New Nations? *AH1*, Issue 9

Was Antebellum Reform Motivated Primarily by Humanitarian Goals? *AH1*, Issue 11

Was the Antebellum South a Unique Section in American History? *AH1,* Issue 15

Social history, Twentieth Century
Did the Women's Movement Die in the 1920s? *AH2,* Issue 10
Was the New Deal an Effective Answer to the Great Depression? *AH2,* Issue 11

Social inequality. *See* **Social discrimination**

Social interaction
Are There Limits to Confidentiality?. *Bio,* Issue 8
Is Urban Life Crazy? *Soc,* Issue 4
Should Children Learn Morality Primarily by Examining Their Own Reasoning? *Psy,* Issue 9
Should One Always Follow One's Conscience? *Mor,* Issue 4

Social security systems
Does Welfare Do More Harm Than Good? *Soc,* Issue 13
Is America Headed for an Economic Bust? *Soc,* Issue 20
Should Immigration Be More Limited? *Soc,* Issue 16

Social stratification
Does "Lower-Class" Culture Perpetuate Poverty? *Soc,* Issue 2
Should Literacy Be Based on Traditional Culture? *Edu,* Issue 14

Social welfare programs
Does Our Welfare System Hurt the Poor? *Pol,* Issue 14
Does Society Have an Obligation to Care for the Less Well Off? *Mor,* Issue 16
Does Welfare Do More Harm Than Good? *Soc,* Issue 13
Is The Welfare System Causing Poverty? *Eco,* Issue 13

Socialization
Is Urban Life Crazy? *Soc,* Issue 4
Was Conflict Unavoidable Between Native Americans and Colonists? *AH1,* Issue 2

Sociology
Is It Wrong to "Politicize" Sociology? *Soc,* Issue 1

Is Population Control the Key to Preventing Environmental Deterioration? *Env,* Issue 6

Soviet-American relations. *See* **United States–Soviet Union relations**

South Africa, Republic of
Is the Pain and Suffering Associated with Disinvestment and Sanctions Worth It for Black South African Workers? *Eco,* Issue 18
Should Strict Sanctions Be Applied Against South Africa? *WP,* Issue 4

South America *See also* Latin America
Should the Less Developed Countries Pay Their International Debts? *WP,* Issue 11
Will the Third World Pay Its Debt? *Eco,* Issue 17

Soviet Union
Could NATO Forces Withstand a Conventional Attack by the Warsaw Pact? *WP,* Issue 12
Does Morality Require Nuclear Disarmament? *Mor,* Issue 18
Does the Soviet Union Truly Want International Cooperation? *WP,* Issue 6
Is Nuclear Deterrence Irrational? *Soc,* Issue 17
Is the End of the Cold War in Sight? *Pol,* Issue 19
Should Superpower Strategic Arsenals Be Cut in Half? *WP,* Issue 13

Special interest groups. *See* **Interest groups**

Standard of living
Is It Time to Abolish the Minimum Wage? *Eco,* Issue 9
Is the Middle Class Shrinking? *Eco,* Issue 19
Was City Government in Late Nineteenth-Century America a "Conspicuous Failure"? *AH2,* Issue 6

START
Could NATO Forces Withstand a Conventional Attack by the Warsaw Pact? *WP,* Issue 12
Should Superpower Strategic Arsenals Be Cut in Half? *WP,* Issue 13

State government
Are There Too Many Hostile Takeovers? *Eco,* Issue 5

Constitution, The: Was It an Economic
Document? *AH1*, Issue 7
Does Government Have a Right to
Prohibit Homosexual Acts? *Pol*,
Issue 15
Do We Need New Federal Legislation to
Protect the Future Integrity of Our
Groundwater? *Env*, Issue 16
Is Measurement-Driven Instruction
Desirable? *Edu*, Issue 15
Is the Legal Profession Declining? *Leg*,
Issue 5
Should Capital Punishment Be
Abolished? *CR*, Issue 13, *Mor*, Issue 11
Should the Death Penalty Be
Abolished? *Leg*, Issue 14
Should the State Require All Family
Life Education Programs to Stress
Premarital Chastity and Monogamy?
HS, Issue 15
Was Reconstruction a Total Failure?
AH1, Issue 17, *AH2*, Issue 1

Stock market
Did Monetary Policy Cause the Stock
Market Crash of 1987? *Eco*, Issue 15
Do Foreign Investments Threaten U.S.
Economic Independence? *WP*, Issue 9
Is America Headed for an Economic
Bust? *Soc*, Issue 20
Was the New Deal an Effective Answer
to the Great Depression? *AH2*,
Issue 11

Strategic Arms Limitation Treaty. *See*
SALT

Strategic Arms Reduction Treaty. *See*
START

Suicide. *See also* Death and dying
Can Suicide Be Rational? *Psy*, Issue 14
Do We Have a Moral Right to Die? *Mor*,
Issue 6
Will Gun Control Reduce Crime? *CR*,
Issue 15

Supreme Court
Are There Too Many Hostile Takeovers?
Eco, Issue 5
Does Government Have a
Constitutional Right to Prohibit
Certain Kinds of Sexual Conduct? *HS*,
Issue 14
Does Government Have a Right to
Prohibit Homosexual Acts? *Pol*,
Issue 15

Does the Supreme Court Abuse Its
Power? *Pol*, Issue 9
Is Abortion Always Immoral? *Mor*,
Issue 8
Is Abortion Immoral? *Bio*, Issue 1
Is Affirmative Action Constitutional?
Leg, Issue 11
Is Affirmative Action Reverse
Discrimination? *Pol*, Issue 12, *Soc*,
Issue 10
Is Capital Punishment Justified? *Pol*,
Issue 11
Is Church-State Separation Being
Threatened? *Edu*, Issue 5
Is It Unconstitutional to Discriminate
Against Homosexuals? *Leg*, Issue 7
Is the Antiabortion Movement Based on
a Belief in the Sacredness of Human
Life? *HS*, Issue 11
Should Capital Punishment Be
Abolished? *CR*, Issue 13, *Mor*, Issue 11
Should Handguns Be Banned? *Leg*,
Issue 16
Should Plea Bargaining Be Abolished?
Leg, Issue 3
Should Pornography Be Protected by
the First Amendment? *Leg*, Issue 10
Should Prayer Be Permitted in Public
Schools? *Leg*, Issue 8
Should the Death Penalty Be
Abolished? *Leg*, Issue 14
Should the Exclusionary Rule Be
Abolished? *Leg*, Issue 15
Should There Be a Right to Abortion?
Leg, Issue 9
Should We Have a "Wall of Separation"
Between Church and State? *Pol*,
Issue 17

— T —

Tax structure
Can Federal Budget Deficits Be Good
for the Economy? *Eco*, Issue 14
Does Welfare Do More Harm Than
Good? *Soc*, Issue 13
Is Tax Reform an Impossible Dream
Come True? *Eco*, Issue 12
Were the Populists Democratic
Reformers? *AH2*, Issue 5

Technological innovation
Can Computers Think? *Psy*, Issue 8

Does the Soviet Union Truly Want International Cooperation? *WP*, Issue 6

Do Patients Have a Right to Die? *Leg*, Issue 13

Do Surrogate Motherhood Contracts Exploit Women? *HS*, Issue 18

Is It Ethical to Withhold the Truth From Dying Patients? *Bio*, Issue 4

Is It Wrong to Create Test-Tube Babies? *Bio*, Issue 2

Is "Killing" the Same as "Letting Die"? *Bio*, Issue 5

Is Nuclear Power Safe and Desirable? *Env*, Issue 8

Is Population Control the Key to Preventing Environmental Deterioration? *Env*, Issue 6

Is the United States Becoming Too Friendly with China? *WP*, Issue 1

Municipal Waste: Is Modern Incineration Technology an Environmentally Benign Alternative to Garbage Dumps? *Env*, Issue 14

Should Organ Procurement Be Based on Voluntarism? *Bio*, Issue 15

Should Schools Serve National Economic Needs? *Edu*, Issue 8

Should We Send Convicts to Penal Colonies? *CR*, Issue 16

Was City Government in Late Nineteenth-Century America a "Conspicuous Failure"? *AH2*, Issue 6

Television. *See also* **Media**

Do the News Media Have a Liberal Bias? *Pol*, Issue 4

Have American Political Parties Lost Their Power? *Pol*, Issue 2

Should Morality and Human Rights Strongly Influence Foreign Policymaking? *WP*, Issue 15

Terrorism

Can Military Action Reduce International Terrorism? *WP*, Issue 14

International Law: Should the United States Expel the PLO's Mission to the United Nations? *WP*, Issue 17

Should Israel Agree to the Creation of a Palestinian State? *WP*, Issue 5

Test-tube babies. *See* **In vitro fertilization**

Therapy. *See* **Psychotherapy**

Third World. *See also* **Latin America; Underdeveloped countries**

Can the Revolution Serve as a Developmental Model for Third World Nations Today? *AH1*, Issue 6

Does the Soviet Union Truly Want International Cooperation? *WP*, Issue 6

Do Rich Nations Have an Obligation to Help Poor Nations? *Mor*, Issue 17

Is the Third World Responsible for Its Own Lack of Economic Development? *WP*, Issue 10

Is the United Nations a Beneficial Organization? *WP*, Issue 18

Should Immigration Be More Limited? *Soc*, Issue 16

Should the Less Developed Countries Pay Their International Debts? *WP*, Issue 11

Will the Third World Pay Its Debt? *Eco*, Issue 17

Toxic chemicals

Are Environmentalists and Industrial Leaders Becoming Less Adversarial? *Env*, Issue 5

Does the Montreal Ozone Agreement Signal a New Era of International Environmental Statesmanship? *Env*, Issue 18

Do We Need New Federal Legislation to Protect the Future Integrity of Our Groundwater? *Env*, Issue 16

Hazardous Waste: Can Present Regulatory and Voluntary Efforts Solve Disposal and Clean-up Problems? *Env*, Issue 13

Is Immediate Action Necessary to Minimize Potential Catastrophic Effects of Global Climatic Warming? *Env*, Issue 17

Is Immediate Action Needed to Combat the Effects of Acid Rain? *Env*, Issue 11

Is There a Cancer Epidemic Due to Industrial Chemicals in the Environment? *Env*, Issue 10

Is the Widespread Use of Pesticides Required to Feed the World's People? *Env*, Issue 9

Municipal Waste: Is Modern Incineration Technology an Environmentally Benign Alternative to Garbage Dumps? *Env*, Issue 14

Nuclear Waste: Was Yucca Mountain an Appropriate Site for Nuclear Waste Disposal? *Env*, Issue 15

Should Regulation of Airborne Toxins Under the Clean Air Act Be Strengthened? *Env*, Issue 7

Should Women Be Excluded from Jobs That Could Be Hazardous to a Fetus? *Env*, Issue 12

Toxic waste. *See* **Hazardous waste; Toxic chemicals**

Trade

Do Foreign Investments Threaten U.S. Economic Independence? *WP*, Issue 9

Is the United States Becoming Too Friendly with China? *WP*, Issue 1

Is the United States in a Period of Decline? *AH2*, Issue 16

Should Strict Sanctions Be Applied Against South Africa? *WP*, Issue 4

Should the United States Protect Domestic Industries from Foreign Competition? *Eco*, Issue 16

Was the Conflict Between the United States and Russia Inevitable? *AH2*, Issue 12

Will the Canada-U.S. Free Trade Agreement Be Beneficial? *WP*, Issue 8

— U —

Underdeveloped countries. *See also* **Latin America**

Is the Third World Responsible for Its Own Lack of Economic Development? *WP*, Issue 10

Should the Less Developed Countries Pay Their International Debts? *WP*, Issue 11

Will the Third World Pay Its Debt? *Eco*, Issue 17

Unemployment

Does Our Welfare System Hurt the Poor? *Pol*, Issue 14

Does Society Have an Obligation to Care for the Less Well Off? *Mor*, Issue 16

Do Firms Exploit Workers and Local Communities By Closing Profitable Plants? *Eco*, Issue 7

Is The Welfare System Causing Poverty? *Eco*, Issue 13

Was the New Deal an Effective Answer to the Great Depression? *AH2*, Issue 11

Unions. *See* **Labor force**

United Nations

International Law: Should the United States Expel the PLO's Mission to the United Nations? *WP*, Issue 17

Is the United Nations a Beneficial Organization? *WP*, Issue 18

United States–China relations

Is the United Nations a Beneficial Organization? *WP*, Issue 18

Is the United States Becoming Too Friendly with China? *WP*, Issue 1

United States military. *See* **Military**

United States–Soviet Union relations

Could NATO Forces Withstand a Conventional Attack by the Warsaw Pact? *WP*, Issue 12

Does Morality Require Nuclear Disarmament? *Mor*, Issue 18

Does the Soviet Union Truly Want International Cooperation? *WP*, Issue 6

Do U.S. Allies Share the Defense Burden Fairly? *WP*, Issue 2

Is American Intervention in Latin America Justified? *Pol*, Issue 18

Is Nuclear Deterrence Irrational? *Soc*, Issue 17

Is the End of the Cold War in Sight? *Pol*, Issue 19

Is the United Nations a Beneficial Organization? *WP*, Issue 18

Is the United States a Declining Power? *WP*, Issue 7

Is the United States Becoming Too Friendly with China? *WP*, Issue 1

Is U.S. Intervention in Latin America and Elsewhere Justified? *WP*, Issue 3

Should Superpower Strategic Arsenals Be Cut in Half? *WP*, Issue 13

Was the Conflict Between the United States and Russia Inevitable? *AH2*, Issue 12

United States–Third World relations. *See also* **Latin America; Third World**

Do Rich Nations Have an Obligation to Help Poor Nations? *Mor*, Issue 17

Is the United Nations a Beneficial Organization? *WP*, Issue 18

Is the United States a Declining Power?
WP, Issue 7

Is U.S. Intervention in Latin America
and Elsewhere Justified? *WP*, Issue 3

Upper class

Does an Elite Rule America? *Soc*,
Issue 11

Does Society Have an Obligation to
Care for the Less Well Off? *Mor*,
Issue 16

Is America Ruled by an Elite? *Pol*,
Issue 1

Is Crime Created by Society's Elites?
CR, Issue 2

Was the Antebellum South a Unique
Section in American History? *AH1*,
Issue 15

Urbanization

Did the Progressives Fail? *AH2*, Issue 7

Is Urban Life Crazy? *Soc*, Issue 4

Should the Police Do More to Manage
Street Life? *Leg*, Issue 4

Was City Government in Late
Nineteenth-Century America a
"Conspicuous Failure"? *AH2*, Issue 6

Was John D. Rockefeller a "Robber
Baron"? *AH2*, Issue 2

Were the Immigrants' Old World
Cultures Destroyed as They Adjusted
to American Life? *AH2*, Issue 4

— V —

Vietnam War

Could the United States Have
Prevented the Fall of South Vietnam?
AH2, Issue 14

Does an Elite Rule America? *Soc*,
Issue 11

Violence

Can Military Action Reduce
International Terrorism? *WP*, Issue 14

Does Pornography Promote Sexual
Violence? *HS*, Issue 13

Do We Need More Jails? *CR*, Issue 14

Is Pornography Harmful? *Psy*, Issue 17

Is Rape Motivated by Aggression
Instead of Sex? *HS*, Issue 12

Is Street Crime More Serious Than
White-Collar Crime? *CR*, Issue 4

Is the Antiabortion Movement Based on
a Belief in the Sacredness of Human
Life? *HS*, Issue 11

Is the United Nations a Beneficial
Organization? *WP*, Issue 18

Is Urban Life Crazy? *Soc*, Issue 4

Should Israel Agree to the Creation of a
Palestinian State? *WP*, Issue 5

Should Morality and Human Rights
Strongly Influence Foreign
Policymaking? *WP*, Issue 15

Should Prostitution Be Decriminalized?
HS, Issue 17

Was Conflict Unavoidable Between
Native Americans and Colonists? *AH1*,
Issue 2

Will Gun Control Reduce Crime? *CR*,
Issue 15

Voting. *See* **Elections**

— W —

War. *See also* **names of specific wars
or conflicts**

Could NATO Forces Withstand a
Conventional Attack by the Warsaw
Pact? *WP*, Issue 12

Could the United States Have
Prevented the Fall of South Vietnam?
AH2, Issue 14

Did Woodrow Wilson Fail as
Commander-in-Chief During World
War I? *AH2*, Issue 9

Should Israel Agree to the Creation of a
Palestinian State? *WP*, Issue 5

Should the U.S. Congress Limit the
President's War Powers? *WP*, Issue 16

Was Conflict Unavoidable Between
Native Americans and Colonists? *AH1*,
Issue 2

Was U.S. Foreign Policy in the Early
Nineteenth Century Imperialistic?
AH1, Issue 12

Waste disposal. *See* **Hazardous waste**

Water pollution. *See also* **Pollution**

Are Environmentalists and Industrial
Leaders Becoming Less Adversarial?
Env, Issue 5

Do We Need New Federal Legislation to
Protect the Future Integrity of Our
Groundwater? *Env*, Issue 16

Water shortage
Do We Need New Federal Legislation to Protect the Future Integrity of Our Groundwater? *Env*, Issue 16
Hazardous Waste: Can Present Regulatory and Voluntary Efforts Solve Disposal and Clean-up Problems? *Env*, Issue 13
Is Immediate Action Needed to Combat the Effects of Acid Rain? *Env*, Issue 11
Municipal Waste: Is Modern Incineration Technology an Environmentally Benign Alternative to Garbage Dumps? *Env*, Issue 14

Wealth
Does an Elite Rule America? *Soc*, Issue 11
Does Society Have an Obligation to Care for the Less Well Off? *Mor*, Issue 16
Do Rich Nations Have an Obligation to Help Poor Nations? *Mor*, Issue 17
Is America Ruled by an Elite? *Pol*, Issue 1
Was the Antebellum South a Unique Section in American History? *AH1*, Issue 15
Was John D. Rockefeller a "Robber Baron"? *AH2*, Issue 2

Welfare. See Social security systems; Social welfare programs

Wildlife
Does Wilderness Have Intrinsic Value? *Env*, Issue 1
Do We Need More Stringently Enforced Regulations to Protect Endangered Species? *Env*, Issue 2
Is It Ethical to Implant Animal Hearts in Humans? *Bio*, Issue 12
Should Animal Experimentation Be Permitted? *Bio*, Issue 14

Women's issues
Can Women Combine Careers and Families? *Soc*, Issue 6
Did the Women's Movement Die in the 1920s? *AH2*, Issue 10
Did Women Achieve Greater Autonomy in the New Nation? *AH1*, Issue 9
Does Good Sex Require Love? *HS*, Issue 4
Does Pornography Promote Sexual Violence? *HS*, Issue 13

Does Welfare Do More Harm Than Good? *Soc*, Issue 13
Do Surrogate Motherhood Contracts Exploit Women? *HS*, Issue 18
Has the Women's Movement Increased Female Criminality? *CR*, Issue 7
Is Abortion Immoral? *Bio*, Issue 1
Is Affirmative Action Constitutional? *Leg*, Issue 11
Is Affirmative Action Morally Justified? *Mor*, Issue 14
Is "Comparable Worth" Worthless? *Eco*, Issue 4
Is Economic Inequality Beneficial to Society? *Soc*, Issue 8
Is It Time to Abolish the Minimum Wage? *Eco*, Issue 9
Is Pornography a Threat to Society? *Mor*, Issue 12
Is Pornography Harmful? *Psy*, Issue 17
Is Rape Motivated by Aggression Instead of Sex? *HS*, Issue 12
Is The "New Woman" the Main Cause of Turmoil and Tension in Male/Female Relations Today? *HS*, Issue 2
Is The Sexual Revolution Over? *HS*, Issue 1
Is the Victims' Rights Movement Succeeding? *CR*, Issue 18
"New Woman," The: Has She Confused Sex Roles? *Soc*, Issue 7
Should Congress Guarantee U.S. Workers the Right to Parental Leave? *Eco*, Issue 8
Should There Be a Right to Abortion? *Leg*, Issue 9
Should Women Be Excluded from Jobs That Could Be Hazardous to a Fetus? *Env*, Issue 12
Should Workers Be Paid According to "Comparable Worth"? *Pol*, Issue 13
Was the Colonial Period a "Golden Age" for Women in America? *AH1*, Issue 3

Working women. See Women's issues

— Y —

Youth
Are Packaged Discipline Programs Harmful? *Edu*, Issue 16
Is The Welfare System Causing Poverty? *Eco*, Issue 13

— Z —